CHRIS STOKEL-WALKER

African Lions

The colonial geopolitics of Africa's gas and oil

ABOUT THE AUTHOR

Chris Stokel-Walker is a 21-year old from Newcastle, England, who has written on such diverse subjects as YouTube, modern art and fruit and veg for a variety of magazines. *African Lions* is his first book, the product of a day in the office for Tethra Energy without the internet.

NIGERIA GAS
HYDROCARBONS

OIL ANGOLA
EQUATORIAL GUINEA

MAURITANIA
GHANANIAN
COLONIALISM

AFRICAN LIONS:

THE COLONIAL GEOPOLITICS OF AFRICA'S GAS & OIL

UGANDA

TERROR

CORRUPTION

CHRIS STOKEL-WALKER

HOPE

Published by Lulu

First published 2011

10 7 4 2 1 5 9 6 3 8

Set in 11-point Palatino Linotype and Franklin Gothic

A CIP catalogue record for this book is available from the British Library

978-1-445-79456-3

www.africanlionsbook.com

For my parents, grandparents,
and Tash.

"And in that moment he was reminded why he
wanted to write in the first place. It's for the same
reason anyone does anything: to impress women."

- Aaron Sorkin

Contents

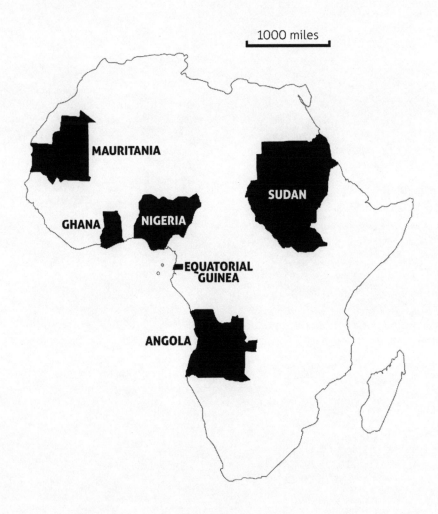

1000 miles

MAURITANIA

GHANA

NIGERIA

SUDAN

EQUATORIAL
GUINEA

ANGOLA

Introduction

"A fundamental principle appears to have been forgotten or overlooked in our system of colonial policy – that of colonial dependence. To give a colony the forms of independence is a mockery; she would not be a colony for a single hour if she could maintain an independent station."

– Sir Edward Cust, 'Reflections on West African Affairs, addressed to the Colonial Office', 1839

The Port Harcourt Military Hospital is a crumbling, fading old building that often suffers terrible power cuts that mean patients are treated at night by the dim glow of candlelight. It sits on the old Aba Road in Port Harcourt, a tarmac road that fades into dusty pavements and low-slung buildings at its edges. Originally called the Delta Clinic, the hospital was built as part of a joint venture by Shell and BP to provide medical care in luscious grounds for its expatriate and local workers that manned the oil rigs the company sprung up all over the Niger Delta.

During the Nigerian Civil War (1967-70) the Delta Clinic was requisitioned by the military along with other key buildings in Port Harcourt and became its triage facility for wounded soldiers in the fight against fellow Nigerians. Since falling into the hands of the military, the once-new hospital has barely seen a lick of paint, never mind a new accident and emergency unit.

It seems likely that members of Nigeria's Joint Task Force, a specialist military hit squad that has been tasked by President Goodluck Jonathan to take the fight to separatist fighters of the Movement for the Emancipation of the Niger Delta (MEND), would be taken to the Military Hospital for treatment to their wounds sustained by the brutal guerrilla fighting on the Niger Delta.

Goodluck Jonathan has an election to win later in 2011, after all, and needs to be seen to be strong in the face of severe opposition to one-sided foreign investment and rapacious drilling of Nigeria's plentiful gas and oil supplies. The freedom fighters of MEND are looking for a change in the way Nigeria treats its most valuable natural resources – an industry that provides a huge proportion of the country's annual income – so that funds are diverted towards local and national pockets, rather than those of international oil and gas companies. A staggering figure couched in a report by the African Development Bank and the African Union[1] found that if funds over the past 50 years of Nigeria's history as an oil producer had found their way into the public purse, rather than the pockets of corrupt leaders, its human and physical capital development would be 400% greater than it now currently is. The potential losses for gas are no better: Nigerian officials' refusal to end the practice of gas flaring, where associated gas from oil production is burnt, rather than collected and sold (a practice which initially began being wound down for environmental concerns, rather than the recognition of profit) has cost them a monumental $150 billion – and they are estimated to still be losing $2.5 billion every year through the practice.[2] Millions of Africans across tens of countries that each also are finding that the promise of hydrocarbons are luring a second wave of colonisers to their countries are equally concerned that their governments are sleepwalking into a new era of being in thrall to the west, and making themselves known through disquiet and outright protest.

Gunshot wounds have become the norm for doctors at Port Harcourt as the battle rages on across the Niger Delta between militants and military. Members of the Joint Task Force are brought in almost daily as they gain flesh wounds sweeping across the difficult swampy terrain in their attempt to force MEND militants out of their foxholes by sheer armed force. Blood suppurates from wounds that the underpaid, overworked doctors rapidly try to close up at the same rate that oil pulses from the ground and into refineries at scores of drilling sites across the Delta. Here in the hospital, as well as at the drilling platforms that dot the landscape, Nigeria's lifeblood is being taken in the pursuit of profit. The medical staff work quickly and carefully as befits their training, even though as in most sectors across Nigeria – and Africa in general – the infrastructure constantly fails them. More than half of Africans surveyed in the PricewaterhouseCoopers Oil & Gas in Africa 2010 investigation[3] believed that the inadequacy of basic infrastructure would have an increasing impact on their work in the coming three years.

This is a situation repeated across Africa; contagion brought about by the promise of billions of dollars in foreign investment for ailing and developing democracies. The comparative youth and inexperience of most nations in Africa compounds the situation: large sections of the population are being swindled by their representatives, believing that bribery and sequestering of money into private pockets is the way that democracy works in the western world. A smaller section is more cognisant of what is occurring, and worry that it is the politicians who are the naïve ones, not the people. The Kenyan government's financial ministry officials told a parliamentary committee[4] in December 2010 that nearly one-third of its yearly national budget – almost $4 billion – is lost to corruption. Either way the general population are wary and mistrustful of foreign companies, remembering all too well the bloody and uncomfortable aftermath of the first scramble for Africa.

Africa has proved for several decades to be a vital source of oil and gas, but looks now more than ever to be of pressing importance to the world's commodity supplies. With many of the more geographically close conventional supplies now drying out, Africa is proving a relatively untapped market that does not require a reliance on unconventional supplies such as shale gas or coal bed methane (CBM). BP, in its Statistical Review of World Energy for 2010[5], put the continent's untapped oil reserves at 127 billion barrels – 10% of the entire world's bank of oil, and 7.9% of all gas reserves (nearly 15 trillion cubic metres). Not only does Africa have significant reserves of oil and gas, but it is growing at a much faster rate than in the rest of the world. Between 1980 and 2006, world oil reserves increased at an average annual rate of 1.7%; reserves in the OPEC group of oil producing countries grew less than that – at 1.5%. African reserves, ignited by a strong focus on exploration, grew annually by 3.2%, double the world average.[6]

Additionally, innovations in technology such as LNG – where gas is supercooled into liquid form at -162°C[7], making it easier to transport – have meant that it is often cheaper and more economical to rely on African LNG to supply western markets. Even with the built-in problem that there is a 'boiling off' process (whereby 0.15% of the cargo contained on LNG vessels evaporates naturally each day), a two week charter from Africa to markets in the USA will still only lose 2% of its cargo, allowing it to take advantage of arbitrage opportunities and a stronger demand overseas. World use of LNG is becoming more widespread – latest figures indicate that more than one-fifth of the world's natural gas is liquefied and shipped to market[8] – and Africa is at the forefront of the LNG industry. Shell have stepped up spending in the region, planning to pump between $25 and $27 billion in projects to 2020[9], which would increase its gas production from its current level of 3.5 million barrels of oil to 3.7 million barrels of oil per day by 2014. Mounir Bouaziz, Shell's Vice President for the Middle East and North Africa, claims that LNG is becoming the default choice for the company to move gas out of Africa. "To put a pipeline in place a very robust security of supply is needed," he said. "LNG however has become the default way of supplying markets with natural gas. Cheap regasification facilities have popularised LNG imports, and there is a growing list of importing countries, which account for 30% of new growth in the gas arena." Britain is rapidly set to become – with its long list of regasification projects tabled for construction – the world's fifth largest LNG importer behind Japan, the USA, South Korea and Spain, and African LNG is almost certain to make up a large percentage of the cargoes delivered to the UK.[10] Currently Nigeria alone, the largest petrostate in Africa, supplies 25% of all Europe's LNG and a staggering 10% of the world's supply. The country's gas export potential, mostly through LNG, could rise to 55 billion cubic metres (bcm) per year, according to Business Monitor International figures.[11]

Even with these large shares of world supply, Africa's ratio of reserves to production is much higher than anywhere else in the world. By dividing the two figures statisticians can extrapolate the number of years current proved reserves would last based on a consistent contemporary production rate. While the world has only 62.8 years of reserves remaining were no more gas to be found and production to continue at today's rates (and North America only a miniscule 11.3 years), Africa would be able to continue for nearly 10 more years than the world average – 72.4 in total. This preferential reserves to production rate is a self-fulfilling cycle too: companies are being drawn towards the continent by its favourable ratio, and exploring with more vigour, constantly finding reserves which prolong the shelf life of the continent as a gas and oil producer.

International companies are therefore moving more actively towards African oil and gas. The continent has always been on the fringes of production, with America and the UK relying initially on domestic production to sate their demand, then as that was expended moving towards local but foreign supply sources via pipeline and topping up any supply shortfalls with African gas. However now, as those sources of supply are running out, Africa is becoming pivotal in supplying the west with cheap and plentiful oil and gas (18% of the total of US oil imports originate on the continent[12]), resulting in a second race to the commodity hidden beneath the continent.

Africans' fears are that this will become a second wave of colonisation, with international oil conglomerates buying up vast swathes of land, shipping in large numbers of foreign contractors and running countries dry with little-to-no care for the local inhabitants, or any employment prospects for local workers. This disquiet manifests itself in unhappiness through the few local people that do manage to find jobs at foreign-owned ventures. At the start of December 2010, when large sections of the world were experiencing a vicious cold snap, local Nigerian workers attached to the Pengassan union at ExxonMobil's headquarters in Lagos and its unit in Eket went on "indefinite strike"[13], according to local branch chairman Jude Nwaogu. "No work is going on," he said. "If management allows this strike to degenerate, we shall pull out our members from the oil platforms and stop oil loading at the terminal." That the tankers which take the produced and supercooled LNG from various ports in Africa to Europe, the United Kingdom and the US are following the self-same Atlantic shipping routes that West African commodity liners took in the heyday of the European empires' stranglehold over the continent does not help the perception in Africa that oil and gas drilling has the potential to benefit everyone but them.

Much like the hive industries that popped up during the first wave of colonialism such as sugar refineries, so LNG facilities have begun to cover the African landscape. The list of existing and planned liquefaction and regas terminals is long already and is ever-growing as the west turns away from its existing supply sources and towards the comparatively untouched haven of Africa.

Already standing today are the Sonatrach and Bethioua LNG plants in Algeria; Bonny LNG in Nigeria; SEGAS Damietta and ELNG IDCO LNG in Egypt and EG LNG in Malabo, Guinea. The 5.2 million tonne per year plant Angola LNG will begin exporting gas from a 240 hectare site at Soyo in 2012, the country's Oil Minister Jose Maria Botelho de Vasconcelos has said, and regas facilities are planned for the following year in Kenya (Mombasa) and South Africa (Mossel Bay and Coega LNG).[14]

Floating LNG facilities berth near African ports to move gas from those countries that have not yet invested in permanent infrastructure and take their gas away to more energy-hungry markets. A 30 billion cubic metres (bcm) per year gas pipeline, the Trans-Saharan or NIGAL pipe, has been planned since the 1970s to provide a gas corridor from Africa to Europe, via Italy. The GALSI (Gasdotto Algeria Sardegna Italia) pipeline incorporated itself as a company in Italy in 2008 and looks to build its pipeline in the coming years, taking gas the same rough route as the Trans-Saharan pipeline.

Sonatrach has built the Medgaz pipeline at a cost of €900 million and began pumping gas into the pipe in late November 2010. When complete and running at full capacity, the pipeline will transport 8 billion cubic metres (bcm) a year from Algeria into Spain, where it can then be moved by internal European pipelines to the rest of the continent.

The Pedro Duran Farell pipeline (known before its renaming as the Maghreb-Europe gas pipeline) was built in the mid-1990s and runs from Algeria to Spain via Morocco at an average annual capacity of 12 billion cubic metres. The infrastructure to move large quantities of gas and oil from African to Europe and the rest of the world already exists or is well on its way through planning, then. There is no doubt that its stock in the global commodity market is rising, and attention is growing on the area as a feasible and impressive source of energy. However the risk still remains that a dash for gas and oil towards the continent looks like the 19th century race to stake a claim on prime African land, and the shameful colonial carve-up which so angered natives.

There are two polarised approaches on how to deal with Africa that pervade conventional thinking: 'colonial celebratists' and 'colonial apologists'. Colonial celebratists look at past history with the continent and see in its dealings a great deal of sense. To them Africa is still the continent of comparative incivility and as such should be condescended to. Often this viewpoint is not explicitly racist: it comes from a misguided sense that Africans are not able at this current stage to handle the smooth running of a conventional democracy (conveniently overlooking the fact that this is the fault of our colonial rule) and therefore should be treated akin to subjects.

Colonial apologists take the diametrically opposite viewpoint: that our catalogue of horrors should be compensated for through a package of reparations that mean engaging with the continent as if they were a western partner, with western technology and western experience of trade. Both ways of approaching what is appallingly called 'the Africa problem' are reductive and offensive.

An acknowledgement of the colonial past *is* needed: the west forced Africa untold suffering through its colonialism, but because of that it is more imperative than ever that we are not standoffish. Africa does not need to be talked down to, but does sometimes seek advice while being too proud to ask outright. Africa is a growing continent with its own idiosyncratic way of working, and appreciates being met halfway by partners. But to make a big deal of the troubled history between former empire and colony is to overstep the mark and underestimate the development of modern Africa.

In many respects the problem is one of its own creation. Companies, nations and individuals stress on how to approach 'Africa' as if it is one collective mind with the same thoughts. It is an easy mistake to make: Nick Grealy of *No Hot Air* asked for clarification when I questioned him about the potential of Africa. "Define Africa," he wrote. "Algeria and Egypt are totally different economically and culturally from Nigeria and Equatorial Guinea."[15] Africa is indefinable as one single entity, just as one cannot create a common European school of thought, regardless of the aims of the European Union. Its past under colonialism does, however, give most African nations some common ground.

Neither a celebratist nor apologist stance is needed then, but a colonial-mindful one. These events happened in the past, and have some altering on the psyche, much as world wars and any number of events do in the past of western countries. But they are not the predominate marker of a man. An African is an African because they live in Africa, not because they were once colonised. What is needed is the bravery to step out of this conventional thinking on Africa. It proves to be a difficult one, given that at one point a little more than a century ago almost all of Africa was under the control of European countries – only Ethiopia and Liberia managed to escape colonial rule. But we were almost all once living under the auspices of colonialism – "postcoloniality may refer as much to the Roman conquest of Britain and its aftermath as to the more recent historical recovery from the 'scramble for Africa' in the nineteenth century",[16] write Rice and Waugh on the theoretical aspects of postcolonialism, or colonial mindfulness.

It is worth examining postcolonialism as a theoretical concept and explaining some of the key terms to help readers better understand why an awareness of Africa as a postcolonial society is helpful in considering how to approach oil and gas negotiations. Postcolonial theorists look to move beyond the common belief of Africa that still is present in most people's thinking – that of a subjugated, inferior group of people (the 'colonial celebratists' discussed above). Nowhere is that more predominant than in the marking of the western world as the 'first world' and Africa as the 'third world': inherent in these names is a ranking of the west as somehow superior to the third world Africa. This is an idealised aim, as Edward Said, one of the leading postcolonial thinkers, has said. "Domination and inequities of power and wealth are perennial facts of human society. [...] The nations of contemporary Asia, Latin America, and Africa are politically independent but in many ways are as dominated and dependent as they were when ruled directly by European powers"[17] – and so they are. Through the requisitioning of Africa's natural commodities, (predominately western) international oil companies are – in the eyes of the average African – once again colonising their land for natural resources. Avoiding giving the appearance of colonisation must therefore be at the head of any company's concerns when exploring Africa, and being wary to not treat governments as the junior partner in any joint ventures a priority. "What we need to do," Said continues, "is to look at these matters as a network of interdependent histories that it would be inaccurate and senseless to repress, useful and interesting to understand."

One of the key terms used in postcolonialism is 'the Other'. It is the idea that the other world (the first world to Africans, the third world to the west) is mysterious, strange and does things the wrong way, whether it be their religion, their morals or their makeup of power or society. Otherness works both ways: we find the concept of appeasing tribal elders to gain access to land alien, while many Africans find our meritocratic democracies strange and inefficient. The difference is that while the west, because it was the imperialist power in the past, feels no need to adapt to African ways, Africa realises that to succeed with the west, they must adopt some of the west's practices. A sea change is needed in our western approach to Africa, then: we too must adapt and meet Africa halfway, being mindful of how our boisterous colonial past has left an unsavoury opinion of the west wanting control of vital and lucrative natural resources, and a wariness today.

"Too often, we generalise, talking of Africa as if it is one country," writes Marieme Jamme.[18] This book aims to demonstrate the past mistakes made by oil and gas companies which have alienated Africa to the concept of resource exploration, development and production. It also shows the current state of play in several key countries, politically, ideologically and culturally, and how that impacts on any potential developments in their oil and gas sectors, trying to demonstrate the differences between the disparate nations of Africa. However, and perhaps most importantly, it explains the history – both colonial and independent – of the whole continent, and why any company looking to invest in Africa must be aware of the continent's past to ensure success in its present. The circumstances around the innocence, enslavement and freedom that Africa has endured in cycles have irreparably altered the general African psyche (regardless of nation) and its attitude towards business specifically. Oil and gas companies are not necessarily welcome to the politicians in many African countries, never mind the people. By reading this book and learning the events that altered African thinking in each country to its current unique position, and the way that Africans approach foreign investment in light of their unfavourable past, readers can hope better to approach potential negotiations with African governments and drilling companies to broach a better deal, and to ensure you quell the often government-led sabotage and opposition to oil and gas development in their own countries, or simply learn more about a continent that is soon to be central to our continued energy security.

Nigeria, Cameroon and the Niger Delta

"The trouble with Nigeria is simply and squarely a failure of leadership. There is nothing wrong with the Nigerian character. There is nothing wrong with the Nigerian land or climate or water or air or anything else. The Nigerian problem is the unwillingness or inability of its leaders to rise to the responsibility, to the challenge of personal example which are the hallmarks of true leadership."

– Chinua Achebe, *The trouble with Nigeria*

The heart of Africa is undoubtedly Nigeria. United States Assistant Secretary for African Affairs Johnnie Carson has said words to the same effect in February 2010 meetings with international oil and gas companies.[19] The most populous country on the continent, Nigeria holds sway over many of the surrounding nations because of its sheer size and wealth of natural resources. All this is in spite of the fact that major infrastructural problems prevent the country from achieving its full potential – though again that is something inherently African which it shares with its other smaller neighbours. Nigeria holds the world's seventh largest natural gas reserves (which would, according to BP estimates, last into the 22nd century even if no more gas were found at current production rates), and has long held the aim of attaining the headline figure of 40 billion barrels of oil in store to be tapped. According to recent internal estimates, it seems likely that they will achieve this landmark number by 2012 through vigorous exploration, which would mean that the country has almost seven times the amount of oil that Norway, one of Europe's largest reserve holders, does. Alongside the plentiful reserves figure Dr. Emmanuel Egbogah, Nigeria's Special Adviser on Petroleum, is hoping that the country's production facilities can begin pumping out a staggering four million barrels of oil every day by the same date.[20]

"When I said this [at a conference] in India I got a lot of challenges on how Nigeria would be able to produce four million barrels per day when the OPEC (Organisation of Petroleum Exporting Countries) quota for Nigeria is well below two million barrels per day," said Egbogah. "It is our intention to apply to increase our quota accordingly." For several years Nigeria has overproduced oil above its OPEC quota by nearly 700,000 barrels per day.

"In terms of strategy to cope with all this demand," Egbogah continues, "I think our aspiration will very comfortably be accommodated. After the nation's Petroleum Investment Bill

(PIB) has been passed, we will very quickly see that the rig count and others, which will enable us to achieve the target, will pour in.

"We're sitting at a very consistent, very comfortable 3.76 million barrels of production per day," he added. "When the PIB is passed, the rig count will increase. I can see us achieving 40 billion barrels from [a current level of] 38.2 billion barrels. Four million barrels per day is not going to be a tall order for us."

However Egbogah's hinting at the problems the Petroleum Investment Bill has found in its embryonic stage vindicates many people's belief that the goal is a pipe dream. "Many of us are not seeing it from where we are sitting," said ExxonMobil's Gilbert Odior in late 2010. "Looking at the rig count in the region – and the exploration plan – we don't see that drive in the industry to get us to 40 billion barrels in two years." Others, speaking under the condition of anonymity said that Egbogah's seemingly simple assertion raises more questions than it answers. "Production is declining and we need to address that decline; lift it up. The only way to lift it is to involve high investment. But are we positioned for it? Apart from the PIB, do we have the right climate to climb?"

Government had claimed 2005, 2006, 2007 and 2010 would be the years they reached reserves of 40 billion, all without fruition. As expected with most developing economies, while they may sit on a veritable goldmine of resources beyond those many western countries could dream of, the governmental infrastructure and naïveté of what is needed to bring about massive projects such as commoditising their gas and oil reserves is holding up precious foreign investment. The Petroleum Investment Bill will permanently alter the balance between Nigeria and foreign oil investors to the country, fundamentally changing most – if not all – aspects of oil exploration, drilling, production, shipping, refining and export. Financial frameworks will be drafted by the bill, as will a sop to MEND and others by altering the level of indigenous involvement in projects. In short, if legislated correctly, the PIB has the potential double whammy to lure international oil companies into the area in even greater numbers by giving off the impression that Nigerian energy policy is no longer confused and duplicitous, while also appeasing the militia that most violently disrupt the potential harmony of the country's drilling platforms.

As with the ever-postponed reserves goal, however, the Petroleum Bill has been riddled by roadblocks and plagued with problems. Initially tabled in 2008, the national assembly has been thrashing out the details of their united, professional international energy policy to present to the world ever since. Lee Maeba, the chairman of the Nigerian Senate Committee on Petroleum, acknowledged the prevailing international viewpoint on Nigeria's handwringing over the Petroleum Bill when he assured a conference in Cape Town that "the government is no longer taking this as a joke." [21]

Far from being a joke, the delay in formulating a single energy policy for the country is halting lucrative foreign investment in the country. Dozie Nwanna, High Commissioner to the United Kingdom, pointed out the potential losses which are resulting from obfuscation in the assembly.[22] His "commission has a number of proposals from Nigerians and even foreign investors declaring an intention to invest in Nigeria's oil and gas industry. What we have been doing is to direct them to the Nigerian National Petroleum Corporation (NNPC) while we wait for legislation in the industry," he said in November 2010. Gazprom are just one company that have stuck their head above the parapet and pointed out that they will be withholding investment until the legislative terrain was assured. The company is willing and able to pour billions of dollars of money into the country to buy up gas and oil assets, but said they will not do so until the Petroleum Bill is passed and ratified by any government that won the election to be held on 9 April 2011.[23]

CEO of Gazprom Nigeria Vladimir Ilyanin said that once these two assurances have been met, "we'll roll out our plans." He and other international CEOs looking to invest in the country will have been disheartened though by the fact that something as fundamentally important as the country's elections have twice been postponed.

Voters were initially meant to be casting their ballots on the morning of 22 January 2011, but the electoral commission asked to delay the polls until March to reorganise the massive electoral register. That was then pushed to April to allow voters to register electronically, part of a $585 million plan to ensure that the year's elections were not beset with allegations of fraud as previous 'democratic' elections have been (in the 2007 election only a miniscule 10% of the population were given ballot tickets, according to American Assistant Secretary to Africa Carson).

These problems in infrastructure are not the only difficulties which seem to be throwing the democratic process off course. Nigeria's status as a fairly evenly split Muslim-Christian country (Muslims make up half of the population, predominately based in the north of the country, Christians representing 40% of the population, focused around the south) means that there was and still is infighting within the ruling People's Democratic Party (PDP) in the run-up to the election. President Goodluck Jonathan, who claimed that he was only chosen to be Vice President to his predecessor because he was from the Christian Niger Delta[24], took office after the death of the Muslim President Umaru Musa Yar'Adua in 2010. Going by the gentlemen's agreement that Presidential candidates for the PDP alternate between the Muslim north and Christian south every two terms, the PDP candidate for President should be a Muslim. Atiku Abubakar, a Muslim, challenged Jonathan to run for the presidency on the PDP ticket. However Goodluck Jonathan claimed his incumbency allows him to forego convention and campaign again, and did so, throwing his hat into the ring in

September 2010. He resoundly beat Abubakar to represent his party in the final elections, earning more than 70% of the vote.

Democracy hanging on the basis of a handshake agreement between two religious factions within a single party is indicative of how many young democracies in Africa operate – and how they so easily come into difficulties. Nigeria has only been free of military rule for a little over 20 years. Ibrahim Babangida, one of the Muslim candidates for the PDP seeking election in 2010 who stepped aside to support Atiku Abubakar, was military dictator following a coup in 1985, showing that elements (and not even fringe elements) of the old ways remain in the centre of current day politics. The country's last election, in 2007, was the first ever civilian-to-civilian transfer of power – and even that was blighted by accusations of corruption that seemed to have some basis in fact. To expect a modern democracy in the western sense from Nigeria is dangerous; to treat them as a colonial subject is even moreso. What must be recognised is that Nigeria, like many African nations, is slowly making steps away from military rule and being the subject of an empire towards being a functional democracy. They face internal strife, dissent from many quarters and often are not free of corruption (Chinua Achebe wrote in 1984[25] that "the countless billions...poured into our national coffers...would have been enough to launch this nation into the middle-rank of developed nations and transformed the lives of our poor and needy. But what have we done with it? Stolen and salted away by people in power and their accomplices. [...] Embezzled through inflated contracts to an increasing army of party loyalists who have neither the desire nor the competence to execute their contracts"), but most involved do want to be.

Oil and gas companies must take care not to pander too much to any one side. They must neither take an overly aggressive colonising stance in negotiating control of commodities, nor solicit a continuation of bad practices such as corruption, even though often bribery is the only way to progress a project. What companies must also realise is that there is often (especially in Nigeria) a large and defiant resistance to foreign investment that is part based on national pride and part used as cover for more nefarious activity.

Constant as an undercurrent is the fear that Nigerians (and Africans in general) may be sleepwalking into 21st century colonialism of their natural resources. Every world culture is aware of their history. For America the spirit of the Mayflower still lives strong in the lives of most citizens; their children are taught the founding myths, and certain totemic dates in the history of the nation.

In Britain we simultaneously revel in, and wince at, our imperial history. Colonies come and go in a mixture of great triumph and deep shame. The western 'first world' historical tradition is passed on through writing. We read books that distil down grand ideas and massive chunks of time into a couple of hundred pages – as you are doing now with this book. The oral tradition has not been a major part of our dissemination of history for a millennium or more. We were a tribal country then, with poorer literary skills and more emphasis on distinct, close-knit communities.

In Africa many countries are still deeply entrenched in the tribal system. For them history is something that *can* be read, but is more likely spoken and lived.

We in the west have a disconnect from our history because of the medium of transmission; the written page is inert and inactive. It is at best capable of stirring emotion and rekindling the spark of memory; at worst, it is simply ink on paper. It is remote: there is a 'then' and a 'now', two states as distinct in our consciousness as geographically are Africa and Britain.

This is not the case in Africa. There history is passed on through generations by tales of the past, by talking more than reading. It is recalled and relived frequently, and there is a constant connection with the past being lived out in the present.

In Nigeria President Goodluck Jonathan is known for his unique fashion sense. He is rarely seen without his wide-brimmed hat, gold chain and black tunic[26]. *Monocle* magazine write that his choice of clothing "reflect[s] the colonial history of the Niger Delta". Dele Olojede, editor of Nigerian newspaper *Next* is quoted in the magazine as saying "there is certainly nothing African in [his] hat – it was never part of our sartorial tradition." Its wide brim is based on the hats worn by the first Britons to land in Nigeria and colonise the country. Likewise, his long black tunic (which many Nigerians – Igbos in particular – wear) stems from similar long coats with tails that British traders wore when they arrived in the country to exploit its resources. Most ostentatiously, the gold chain – which more than any other item of his apparel has become Jonathan's calling card – has its lineage in the bribes of gold and glass beads feathered onto chains that the British gave to Delta tribal leaders for their tacit support. All three major parts of Jonathan's sartorial look have their roots in the formalwear and gifts that the British colonialists brought to the continent, indicating that even today there is still an indelible link between the country's colonial past and its postcolonial present. The fact that the items are worn as a status symbol makes their effect even more powerful. Not only is Goodluck Jonathan simply cognisant of his nation's history. He is literally living the past in his choice of clothing.

This conscious connection with the past has also altered relationships in the present with oil and gas producers. Nigeria exports precious little of its resources to its former colonial master (the only recent link – and a tenuous one at that – is the Maersk Meridian cargo that arrived in the UK's Isle of Grain LNG facility from the US, whose payload is widely believed to have originated from Nigeria). Rather, it has chosen to favour connections with other European countries that do not have the taint of direct colonial rule over the country. France controlled large swathes of West Africa under its own rule, but never Nigeria. Today it is highly active in the country through companies such as Total SA and Shell (which explains Nigeria's annual 2.69 billion cubic metre (bcm) shipment of LNG to Mexico), who have strong bases in France, Spain and Portugal. Nigeria's shipments to North America may slow, however, by 2015 when its current contracts with Shell lapse. In preparation for this the country has been building – much like other African countries, as will be discussed in more detail below – contacts in the developing markets in Asia and the rest of the world. While currently these LNG exports to China, India, Japan, South Korea and Taiwan only stand at about 3% of its total exports (according to the 2010 BP Statistical Review), the Nigerian government hope that they will increase to replace at a similar rate that others wane lost links in Europe and North America. The country has also brokered a deal with Brazil to export small amounts of LNG (only 80 million cubic metres in 2009, though widespread droughts in Brazil during 2010 led to a steep increase in LNG imports from the previous year to make up the shortfall in energy produced by the country's hydropower plants[27]) which it hopes will flourish as production increases.

The problem is that Nigeria Liquefied Natural Gas (NLNG), the company that exports the near-16 billion cubic metres of LNG annually, is a joint venture between the Nigerian state energy company and foreign investors, including Shell and Total SA. Here lies the inherent problem: international co-operation of some level must always be necessary for African countries in order that they can make the most of their resources. Postcolonialism has a standard cycle according to Said: the western masters dominate, the oppressed rise up. "The triumphant natives soon enough f[in]d that they need the West and that the idea of *total* independence [i]s a national fiction." But with co-operation comes the risk of co-option and losing operating control to foreign investors who are focused purely on self-interest, rather than the benefit of the nation. Thus any approach to co-operation in public-private partnerships must be made with a clear intent that such partnership will be equal at worst, and biased towards Nigeria at best, otherwise suspicion of falling into a casual colonialism may scupper the deal. 'Foreign' in Nigeria is often a byword for money-grabbing and destructive – especially amongst the people and the freedom fighters who claim to represent them.

*   *   *

The terrorist organisation the Movement for the Emancipation of the Niger Delta (MEND) believe they are crusading against the corrupted sort of public-private partnerships that are rife within much of African oil and gas; ostensibly they present themselves as an African Robin Hood-type figure, with a large band of merry men. However the reality is that they are heavily armed, great in number (an October 2009 amnesty by the Nigerian government saw 8,000 of the most peaceable militants come forward to surrender arms, though many are believed to have since found more weaponry and taken up the fight once more) and have a wide spread over Nigeria – and its offshore assets.

While a total and focused written document does not exist, MEND's manifesto – which often changes dependent on the specific hat they choose to wear on each skirmish with the government, whether it be as kidnapper, guerrilla mob or petty thieves – is at its most basic one of freedom and a return of power to the Nigerians. They believe that Nigeria's natural resources have been co-opted by international organisations that hold inordinate sway over a weak government – a claim backed by many observers, including Nick Grealy, who calls Nigeria, alongside Angola and Equatorial Guinea "basically kleptocracies". In a replaying of anti-colonial separatism, MEND believes that the Nigerian people are being cowed by the power of oil and gas explorers, drillers and shippers without seeing any of the gain. They aim to return control of natural resources to the people, retaining the profits from such fields within the country, and to gain compensatory payments from the international oil companies that have ravaged their habitat and left them with a polluted water table, decimated forests and annihilated agriculture.

In reality, while MEND's aims are at first glance laudable, the manner of strongarming the government by kidnapping foreign nationals working on oil rigs and planting explosions at oil and gas refineries links them more to terror groups than a positive movement for action and their policy of piracy and kidnapping has made Nigeria waters "generally risky"[28] to operate in. Lieutenant Colonel Timothy Antigha of the Nigerian Joint Military Task Force said[29] that the group have, "over the years, hijacked an otherwise genuine struggle to feather their own nest. Consequently, the prospect of a quick end to the stand-off in the Niger Delta, employing a combination of military operation and dialogue where necessary, has opened a spectre of loss of revenue, relevance and reckoning." They aim to change the status quo through terror, rather than negotiation; in 2006, they warned international oil companies working in the country that "the Nigerian government cannot protect your workers or assets. Leave our land while you can or die in it."

With this vituperative language, and equally violent actions, MEND is little more than a nascent attempt at a separatist military coup, realising that to the victor in the Nigerian Delta is the spoils: the control over licensing and refining the natural resource which has made even the most secure western democracies envious to the point of violent insurgency. "Our aim," they wrote in the same 2006 email, "is to totally destroy the capacity of the Nigerian government to export oil."

Government has sat up and listened to these stark threats. From inauspicious beginnings in 2006, MEND has risen quickly under the stewardship of Henry Okah to become a major political force in the Delta region, and the nation as a whole: all without running for office. They can rightly claim that their insurgency hits daily Nigerian production by 25% at their most disruptive, costing the government as much as $1 billion each month in lost revenue[30]. They bombed international heads of state at Nigeria's October 2010 Independence Day celebrations in Abuja (and are widely rumoured to have kept Gordon Brown and the Duke of Gloucester away from the parade when they tipped off the British intelligence services to the twin car bombs that killed 12 and injured 17). They push up prices by cutting supplies, and by making it more expensive to pay contractors to head into a warzone to work. Improbable, but not impossible is the rumour that Henry Okah himself is responsible for smuggling a quarter of a million weapons into the country for use by his fighters. They even hold sway over the highest office in the state. Then-President Umaru Musa Yar'Adua bowed to MEND pressure to release two conspirators to the state, Diepreye Alamieyeseigha (a corrupt former Governor of the Bayelsa State) and Mujahid Dokubo-Asari, in 2007.

Alamieyeseigha and Dokubo-Asari were both leaders of the Ijaw, a 15 million-strong subsection of the Nigerian people, who provide many prominent politicians and lawmakers, including current Nigerian President Goodluck Jonathan. Many MEND members are also of the same tribe, showing how much as we will learn later in the example of Mauritania, there is still a level of internecine conflict inherent in Nigeria. While MEND claims that they are one of the more peaceful separatist groups running the Niger Delta, their work to release Dokubo-Asari, who they continue to claim they had and have no connection with, belies that fact.

Prior to his imprisonment ordered by Umaru Musa Yar'Adua, Dokubo-Asari declared foreign oil companies fair game for indiscriminate killings and bombings, rather than the kidnappings and disruptive bombing campaigns that MEND use now to slow down oil production. He even went as far as to suggest that the Niger Delta should secede from the rest of the country and create its own state, under guerrilla rule and martial law. Dokubo-Asari has to date not managed to cement his bid for independence, but his actions, and those of MEND, show that some tribes are more vociferous in their opposition to international oil domination of the Delta than others are. So great is the problem in Nigeria that on taking office in May 2010, Goodluck Jonathan prioritised only three main areas in his very first public address[31] – two of which directly tie in to the oil drilling on the Delta: peace in the area between MEND and international companies, fighting the corruption which blights the area (and nation), and electoral reform.

The 74 ExxonMobil staff working at the Ibeno oil facility offshore the Akwa Ibom state in the Niger Delta would be forgiven for feeling slightly on edge as they went about their daily business on 14 November 2010. Oil plants and rigs are by their nature isolated, often several miles offshore and sometimes hours away from contact with the mainland. That two days earlier MEND had released the names of the seven workers they kidnapped that week and explained in precise detail how they had encountered "stiff resistance from the Nigerian military" but overcame them in an "intense firefight" before attempting to set the High Island VII rig alight would be playing on the minds of those working at all separate rigs. Ibeno was foreign-owned and therefore fair game to the eyes of MEND.

The sun was down at ten o'clock on a Sunday night and the Ibeno facility seemed calm on the surface. Undoubtedly some were worried, however, at recent attacks instigated by MEND – for good reason. The first sign of the attack was the crumpled booms of explosives detonating: they were rigged to the facility itself. Ibeno is one of eight platforms on the Oso field, sitting on a spoil that produces roughly 75,000 barrels of crude oil and 60,000 barrels of natural gas liquid (NGL) every day across all facilities[32]. The use of bullets, never mind heavy explosives, on an oil field is like holding a lit match to a powder keg.

Six speedboats raced alongside the facility and Ibeno was boarded by MEND fighters carrying guns. The boats raised white flags – but not to signify surrender in the western sense. MEND sail under the white flag of Egbesu, an Ijaw water spirit. They believe that they are defending the honour of Egbesu by keeping Delta waters in the control of the Ijaw people, and that by flying under his flag they will be protected from all bullets that come their way. There was a firefight to quell the military guard over the facility, and seven layworkers, all members of the Pengassan oil workers union were taken along with an eighth hostage, a member of management at ExxonMobil. They were whisked away to one of the many militant camps that MEND run on the Delta, some of which have come under protracted government rocket fire as an attempt to smoke out the fighters.

Once there, a statement was prepared and released, much as it had been done for the similar kidnapping the week before at Okoro. Then it had been seven workers on a rig run by the exploration company Afren: two American employees of Transocean, James Robertson and Jeffrey James; the Canadian Robert Croke of PPI; Patrick Weber of Transocean and Mignon Gilles of Sodexo, both French; and the Indonesians Permana Nugraha and Robert Tampubolon, who worked for Century Energy Services.

The statement was chilling for anyone working on a foreign-owned facility: "In the coming weeks we will launch a major operation that will simultaneously affect oil facilities across the Niger Delta." The Ibeno incursion had been a response, MEND claimed, "to the indiscriminate bombing and strafing of communities in the Niger Delta and locations in the creeks and swamps suspected of accommodating militia camps by the Nigerian military. "The Nigerian government to date has refused to enter into dialogue over addressing the injustice in the Niger Delta, preferring instead to deceive the world into believing that the Niger Delta issue has been resolved by the government of Goodluck Jonathan." The government's attempt at an amnesty had not stopped them, they said. All they had done was bribe "a few miscreants." MEND were not going anywhere. Chillingly Jomo Gbomo (a catch-all *nom de guerre* used by most MEND spokespeople) said that "nothing will be spared." If oil companies' employees were harmed during the kidnapping of workers or the attacks on oil facilities, then so be it. To 'Gbomo's' mind, and to the minds of those in MEND, the oil companies, not the militants, would "bear the guilt."

Before the eight kidnapped from Ibeno, before the seven kidnapped from High Island VIII on Okoro, MEND had taken three French citizens and a Thai national from the Bourbon Alexandre, busy working at a field operated by Addax, on 21 September. They were released at the same time as MEND named those taken at Okoro, and just a few days before Ibeno. It appeared to the world that as long as foreign investment was coming into Nigeria, plundering its resources and going out again without leaving investment for the natives, the round of kidnapping would continue as if powered by conveyer. A violent firefight would be followed by a hostage situation, requiring either the beneficence of MEND or the belligerence of Nigerian military might to free them.

The spate of Nigerian kidnappings in the last few months of 2010 are said to be the work of one man: Obese Kuna, a rising general within MEND who has a tighter link towards organised crime than the environmental wings of the group. Obese – real name Tamunotonye Kuna, a 25-year old from the Niger Delta – is one of the precociously young new commanders in the field of an organisation known to be a hodge-podge of different tribal groups fighting for different aims (and with differing levels of morality on how to do so). He was believed to have personally overseen the holding of many of the hostages[33] taken in late 2010 prior to his arrest after being lured into a meeting to negotiate a surrender and despite his criminal links, has treated them well in captivity. With good reason too: in April 2009 Police Inspector General Mike Okiro revealed that between 2006 and 2008 more than $100 million of ransoms were paid to groups like MEND across the whole of Nigeria. Kidnapping not only raises awareness of the plight of those living in the Delta – it bankrolls the continuing fight, too.

MEND have managed to capitalise on the biggest swayer of public opinion across the world. Without exception, irrespective of cultural differences or geographical boundaries, people are affected by fear. If the families of workers on offshore oil rigs believe their loved ones are likely to be kidnapped while they work, they will tell that person their fear. A seed of doubt will be planted in that workers' mind, and soon he will be wary of going to work in Nigeria. The occasional outbursts of violence that come from piracy in the seas around Nigeria (one attack on 30 October 2009 on a ship sailing under Swiss colours saw nine hijackers injure nine crewmembers – three seriously – and the breaking of the Master's fingers when he refused to cooperate[34]) will dissuade workers even more. Without the assurance that their employees can work without being held hostage by heavily armed militants, oil companies begin pulling out of the country. MEND have hit on a tactic which sees their aims likely to succeed. It may not happen today or tomorrow, but sooner rather than later the grinding effect of fear, and the sheer volume of these attacks (80 occurred in 2008 alone[35]), will take hold and MEND will succeed in their aims.

Does that make Nigeria a no-go area for large internationals? *The Economist*'s Operational risk rankings declared Nigeria the 15th most risky of 180 rated countries in its 2010 edition, a worse place to do business than Iran and Pakistan. On the surface, it seems that it would be easier for companies to wash their hands of the area and move to somewhere less fractious, but Africa is one of the few places remaining that has plentiful reserves of conventional oil and gas. Total SA CEO Christophe de Margerie is loath to think about abandoning the country, but is unsure.[36] "The easiest solution is to say," he told investors, "that each time we are confronted with a security problem we should leave, but then there won't be any more oil. If it gets worse, we may have to leave." In order that the world – and Europe especially, who are building ties with North Africa as an alternative to the increasing market domination the Russians are holding over European supplies – is not held in a stranglehold by the whim of some less-than-dependent oil states such as Russia and the Middle East, they must use Africa's plentiful resources. However even MEND admit that Nigeria is "gradually heading towards an abyss of civil war" the likes of which it has sadly experienced in the past. Sully Abu, who was directing Goodluck Jonathan's campaign to be returned President, has said in the past that "Nigeria is like being on an airplane that has just been taken over by hijackers. You do not want to compromise with the gunmen, but the prime concern is to land the plane, so there's no choice but to give in."

There are even accusations of double-dealing that state-level officials and military brass are turning a blind eye to skirmishes for a cut of the ransom money and any stolen machinery. "[The] kidnapping business is a source of fraud for the [regional] governors", a human-rights lawyer named Festus Keyamo told *The New York Times* in 2009[37]. MEND fund their attacks from gun running and petty crime, showing their indelible link to criminality. They also manage to siphon off millions of dollars of oil daily – some estimates believe that up to 10% of all Nigeria's oil is stolen at source by MEND and other gangs. One single raid in December 2010[38] by the Nigerian Joint Task Force seized nearly 14,000 litres of refined crude in almost 700 barrels hoarded by a single small syndicate of locals in Bayelsa State with a value of nearly $10,000. The cumulative effect of these smaller raids, coupled with the more daring (and profitable) ones by those associated with MEND hamstring the Nigerian oil economy at source. The hydrocarbon resources are tithed by criminal gangs automatically, though they have little or nothing to do with the exploration, drilling or refinery of the oil and gas. Without complicity from some rogue officials, such lucrative theft would be nearly impossible; therefore a level of co-operation between MEND and ministers must be assumed.

The government – whether purely superficially or as part of a more concerted effort – are fighting back against MEND. The seven hostages taken from the High Island VIII rig at Okoro and the eight from the ExxonMobil Ibeno facility were freed along with four others as part of a military Joint Task Force exercise that formed part of a larger offensive that looked to quell the MEND resistance in the Bayelsa, Rivers and all-important Delta states. Trumpeting their spoils of war, Nigerian Lieutenant Colonel Timothy Antigha claimed that they had confiscated 30,000 rounds of ammunition, dynamite, an anti-aircraft gun and rocket propelled grenade launchers (RPGs)[39]. The 19 freed men were paraded in front of the press looking dishevelled and blinking from the bright lights of the photographers' flashbulbs and the industrial lighting needed to help news cameras pick up their faces. This was an unmitigated success, the Nigerian army and government said.

The Joint Task Force had launched simultaneous attacks on 14 different camps in the Delta – which tellingly the military were calling "the war zone" – mid-afternoon of 18 November by blocking the creeks that lead to the secluded hideouts in order to prevent any militant escape. Several soldiers and policemen were killed and scores injured as the battle raged on across the vast marshy landmass, with ordinary inhabitants of the Delta being caught in the crossfire. "We have to run for safety," one said, "because bullets are flying all over the place in our communities. We want to avoid stray bullets from killing us."[40] A sustained JTF air bombing raid on the village of Ayakoromo aimed at killing a MEND general killed 150 people in early December 2010 according to estimates by Oghebejabor Ikim, a spokesman for the Forum of Justice and Human Rights Defence. In response to the allegations of a bungled operation, the Joint Task Force's spokesman Timothy Antigha claimed that "only identified camps were targeted. However, the adjoining buildings became part of the JTF targets when fleeing criminals took over the buildings, made them defensive positions and fired at JTF troops." A spokesman for the militants then issued an 'SOS to President Barrack [sic] Obama', declaring "the action of JTF soldiers killing innocent, harmless defenceless civil population an act of terrorism and a mark of self-defeatism in war. Why must a trained soldier point his nozzle at a defenceless woman and release his trigger?"[41]

The heavy-handed nature of the attacks and the chance of being caught in the crossfire were not the only things piquing the anger of those living on the Delta. While many passively support the aims of groups like MEND, those who disagree with the terrorists' tactics and goals were being driven against the military show of strength. Demonstrating how even public entities such as the police and army are considered to be corrupt in many African states, a Colonel Sarhim of the Joint Task Force was compelled to give reporters a tour of one hamlet near the Obotobo-1 camp after word spread amongst residents that the soldiers torched innocent bystanders' houses as well as the militants' camp.

After the fightback, the military brass claimed MEND and other separatist groups were on the back foot, while Nigerian special forces were now launching attacks on MEND bases around the Delta area in order to purge the country of the militants.

The Delta, though, is the size of Portugal. It is full of marshes, trees and rivers that provide cover and battlements for anyone holed up there; for many, "the conditions of rural communities where crude oil is produced are deplorable, with severe environmental degradation, and no access to safe drinking water, electricity and roads. The results have been disillusionment, frustration about their increasing deprivation and deep-rooted mistrust," wrote the United Nations Development Programme in a 2006 report on the region.[42] MEND are a fluid army with no strict internal structure:

affiliated criminals and petty thieves can claim allegiance one day and be gone the next.

Nigerian authorities (or rather a section of those who are believed not to be conspiring with the group, believing also that the nation has been robbed of prosperity from its natural resources because of the group) are fighting the war against MEND the best they can, but ultimately it is a losing battle. It is impossible to fight an army that does not exist in any organised form and impossible too to understand the make-up of a band of fighters from disparate backgrounds and with different aims. Even those supposedly responsible for such attacks squabble over being the first to deny culpability and pass on the blame. General Nikko of the Akwa Ibom State Axis, another militant group who have worked with MEND fighters in the past but laid down arms for President Umaru Musa Yar'Adua's amnesty, has blamed piracy for the November 2010 skirmishes at the ExxonMobil facility in the Akwa Ibom state.[43] "There are no more militants in Akwa Ibom state," Nikko claimed. "All that we see are mere sea pirates who now masquerade as militants to wreak havoc on oil companies." Uncertainty rules when it comes to pinning down who exactly is responsible for the rapid-fire attacks on international oil assets in Nigeria.

This is in part thanks to the sheer size and sweeping scale of Nigeria. It is Africa's most populous country, with more than 120 million people harking from over 250 individual tribes. In the Niger Delta alone, 20 million live on isolated promontories in the swampland and amongst the trees. Community matters in Nigeria, with the tribes the focus of each small geographical region. However the unique terrain of the Delta means that these separate tribes are disconnected yet more from each other, with individuals feeling loyalty to their tribal leaders and their diktats, rather than to the centralised government who often put (and have historically put) unified fiscal gain before the needs of the people in these remote areas.

The Nigerian government has tried to pair the rod with the olive branch, launching a youth training programme aimed at stemming the tide of residents that turn towards the militia for a life and a liveable wage. Samuel Ode, Minister of State for the Niger Delta, claims that the piecemeal road building, housing construction and cleaning projects are making a difference. "All these projects are impacting on the socio-economic life of the people. Young men are working at these sites. I believe that the post-amnesty programme of the Federal Government is something that cannot be executed on a short term basis," he stated defiantly. "Of course, there are quick means and very low-earning fruits, which we intend to tap into to make sure that we offer palliative [treatment], but the main post-amnesty programme is something that should be enduring. It is not something that we should do overnight." The inherent problem is that the youths being wooed by the MEND recruiters are looking for a quick fix to their financial and social straits even moreso than MEND themselves claim they are looking for a long term solution that is beneficial to the future development of the Delta.

To the minds of many MEND proves to be a more potent – and infinitely more seductive – force than the government itself. Though Henry Okah went on the run and was subsequently arrested in Johannesburg the day after the MEND attacks on the Independence Day anniversary parade, where he still remains today, he is despite that more powerful than President Goodluck Jonathan. In a country which has seen equal uncertainty from firm military dictators and weak democratic leaders alike, the choice is simply whether you want your failed leader to have the illusion of strength or not. Okah gives the impression of strength and for many, though responsible for spilling Nigerian blood in more than a half-decade of attacks and corrupt in his own ways, he is preferable to the politicians. "There are thousands of people who are willing to fight and they'll continue to fight [for me],"[44] Okah bragged from prison in December 2010.

Okah's plummy British accent gives away his privileged upbringing in Nigeria's private schools and makes him alluring and cultured. Unlike the politicians who often have the same accent, however, he is fiercely patriotic and not willing to kneel at the hand of the west. His engineering degree means that he has the expertise in the oil and gas industry that many of the politicians tasked with creating the Petroleum Investment Bill simply do not. He made a cottage industry from stolen oil, hiring locals, government officials and military officers ("a senior military officer, when asked [by Chatham House] if oil theft was done by local people, expatriates, military officers or government officials, replied simply: 'All'"[45]) at favourable rates to do the grunt work but paying them fairly – employment that often does not go to native workers when international oil companies come drilling. If you have to work under a corrupt leader, many Nigerians reason, it is best to work under one who looks after his own.

MEND itself came about because of corruption: Delta politicians set up the loose collection of gangs that eventually became MEND to help them rig elections and intimidate voters. Their successes in placing corrupt politicians into power gave them a taste of involvement in the running of regional politics – and an indication of how far a willingness to bend the rules can take you in Nigeria.

The country stands at joint-134th of 178 countries[46] in Transparency International's Corruption Perceptions Index 2010 with a score of 2.4 out of a possible 10 (where 10 is "very clean" and 0 is "highly corrupt"). That places it 28th out of 47 countries in sub-Saharan Africa, and more corrupt than Kosovo (110th: 2.8), Sri Lanka (91st: 3.2) and Colombia (78th: 3.5). More than 45% of the 57 respondents from 16 countries in the PricewaterhouseCoopers African Oil & Gas Survey 2010 believed fraud and corruption would impact on their businesses in the coming three years. An oil fund worth $20 billion in 2007 that was set up by former President Olusegun Obasanjo which held revenues from hydrocarbon exploitation for future needs across the country had dwindled to under $400 million by September 2010, when it should in reality have swelled by a further $10 billion or more per year. $30 billion of revenues from the oil exploration and production in Nigeria had been withdrawn from the fund through infrastructure investment (the main aim of the fund upon its establishment) and regular payments to the governors of various states, of which the government, by their own admission, had little oversight.

There is a common joke in Nigeria, told by Tolu Ogunlesi, the Features Editor for NEXT, the Nigerian daily newspaper[47]. A man dies and goes to hell. Once there, he finds that there is a different hell for each country, so he tries to seek out the least painful one. At the door to German Hell, he is told: "First they put you in an electric chair for an hour. Then they lay you on a bed of nails for another hour. Then the German devil comes in and whips you for the rest of the day."

The man does not like the sound of that, so he checks out American Hell, Russian Hell and many more. They are all similarly gruesome. However, at Nigerian Hell a long line of people is waiting to get in. Amazed, he asks, "What do they do here?"

He is told: "First they put you in an electric chair for an hour. Then they lay you on a bed of nails for another hour. Then the Nigerian devil comes in and whips you for the rest of the day."

"But that's the same as the others," says the man. "Why are so many people waiting to get in?"

"Because of the power cuts, the electric chair does not work. The nails were paid for but never supplied, so the bed is comfortable. And the Nigerian devil used to be a civil servant, so he comes in, signs his time sheet and goes back home for private business."

Corruption has become endemic in the nation, even outside government and the gas and oil industries. Not-for-nothing is Nigeria known as the home of the 419 scam, where millions of emails are sent worldwide asking for a small advance of money to be electronically transferred with the future promise of greater return. Most of these scams are run by young Nigerians, whose abject poverty due to a lack of government investment of oil and gas profits in localities means that they often have a simple choice: online criminal activity, or physical crime under the same gangs that are fighting for the energy independence and self-determinism of the Niger Delta. Corruption is open and flagrant; it has even reached the status of a widespread cultural meme with Nigeria's most famous author, Chinua Achebe basing one of his novels (1960's *No Longer at Ease*) around a young Igbo who struggles to master the intricacies of western democracy when he joins the colonial Nigerian civil service. The protagonist, Obi Okonkwo, is singled out by the community as the shining light – the new promise of Nigeria. He is bankrolled by the Igbo tribe to go to England and study at the bar so that he can come back and help the community pick their way through the western-style colonial culture that was encroaching on the old tribal ways as Nigeria migrated towards a self-sufficient democracy based on wealth from its own land. He, however, becomes susceptible (as many politicians in Nigeria and Africa now still are) to the lures of bribes and corruption, and ends up arrested, derobed and ashamed at how the western way has corrupted him. Indicative of the approach then – and the approach now – comes in the admittance that "you may cause more trouble by refusing a bribe than by accepting it." Earlier, answering directly to the impact of hydrocarbons on the country, Achebe coins a proverbial phrase: "if one finger brings oil it soils the others."[48]

While corruption is rife in the oil and gas industry, the Nigerian authorities claim (on the surface) to be cracking down on it. Anti-fraud police called in 23 representatives of Halliburton and Shell for questioning in December 2010 over bribes paid to all aspects of Nigerian authority, from local tribesmen to government officials[49]. A subsidiary of Halliburton already pleaded guilty to paying $180 million in bribes to Nigerian officials in a US court in 2009, having to pay $579 million in fines because of the bribes, while Shell were forced to pay out $48 million in response to accusations of bribing customs officials in the country. At first glance these seemed to be the first steps towards sifting out corruption in the country. However it rapidly became obvious that it was an opportunist's hope that after the American justice system managed to wring out large amounts of fines from the companies there is a profit to be remade on the original bribes many officials received. The bombast of Femi Babafemi, a Nigerian Economic and Financial Crimes Commission spokesman, declaring that "we are filing charges against [Dick] Cheney" before a volte-face after accepting $250 million "in lieu of prosecution"[50] indicated that the bringing of charges against the former US Vice President and his company was more a money- and PR-grab than root and branch change.

Oil and gas are the locus of corruption in Nigeria, and have been for the 50 years that the Niger Delta has been commercially producing oil. First oil was discovered in the southern Biafra region in 1956. The largely Christian south of the country had been constantly in conflict with the northern Muslim section, with a strong undercurrent of religious tension that took precedence even over the collective dislike of colonial rule that had been in place from 1 January 1901 until Nigeria was granted independence in October 1960. Aside from the simple north-south, Muslim-Christian split that had been longstanding before British rule and was neglected by the colonisers, at the time that Nigeria was granted its Freedom Charter by Britain there were also nearly 300 separate and unique ethnic tribes, each with their own individual beliefs, power systems and customs.

Indeed prior to 1901, Nigeria as a concept did not exist. Each of these tribes held their own territory and involved themselves in skirmishes and pitched battles in order to gain precedence over what was then an uncharted and delineated West Africa. When corralled into a single country with defined boundaries by British overlords, the individual tribes who had their own identities felt suffocated and constrained by their new collective name: Nigerians. Diametrically opposed tribes who had previously existed – while not harmoniously, perhaps manageably – together by keeping their distance and own beliefs were now forced together in thrall of a western ruler who sought to monetise the country for its own gain. It was a situation which would leave the nation a century on in a position that Karl Maier, in his state-of-the-nation book 'This House Has Fallen', described bluntly. Nigeria would become "the bastard child of imperialism, its rich mosaic of peoples locked into a nation-state they had had no part in designing."[51]

Colonial rule, while not ideal for either the north or south of the country, suited the Christian southern tribes more than the Muslim north. The south began to move towards a westernised system of democracy, while the north remained entrenched in its ways. One key problem was that – as today – the Muslim north held the dominant slice of the population. While the north was worried that the Christian south were growing too close to their colonial rulers and would come to dominate the ruling of the country, forcing them into Christian practices, so the southern tribal leaders were concerned that simple mathematics would mean that their beliefs would be subsumed into a Muslim ruling majority. In the late 1940s and early 1950s the southern Christian tribes asked their British rulers for independence and a return to the pre-colonial days where Nigeria would be divided into smaller states, each with their own seat of power, in an attempt to avoid Muslim domination from the (comparatively united) north. The British rejected the request, recognising that dividing the country into independent states would also mean that the country's commodities would be carved up and result in an oil war.

The British washed their hands of the country in October 1960 by giving them independence. For five years the fledgling democracy stuttered along until a military coup, under the directorship of Lieutenant Kaduna Nzeogwu (a northern commander) placed General Johnson Aguiyi-Ironsi (the southern Igbo head of the army) into power as President of Nigeria. Once he had gained power, the new President double-crossed his northern partners and instituted a policy of ethnic cleansing of Muslims, annexing control for the southern representatives.

The northern commanders rallied in July 1966 and placed a northern Christian commander, Lieutenant Colonel Yakubu Gowon into the Presidency as an attempt to compromise with the ousted south and stop the cycle of conflict. By now, however, tensions had been ramped up to such a state that ethnic conflict was unavoidable. As revenge for the southern Igbo President Aguiyi-Ironsi killing northerners, President Gowon began the systematic killing of any Christian Igbo living in the north. 30,000 were butchered and 1.8 million Igbo living until then in the north fled to the relative safety of the south.

Before the northern commanders under Gowon could annex and raid the now-lucrative Biafra region, awash with oil, Lieutenant Colonel Odumegwu Ojukwu seceded from Nigeria. The Republic of Biafra was established at the end of May 1967, distinct from the Federal Government of Nigeria that was still essentially a northern military dictatorship. The southern breakaway Republic had been voted on by assembly, and as such was recognised by the Ivory Coast, Haiti, Zambia and other countries, and received support – but not recognition as a state – from the Vatican, Israel, France and Portugal. Tellingly (and perhaps counterintuitively, given previous northern fears that the south was cosying up to Britain) the former colonial rulers of Nigeria pledged their support to the north, alongside the USSR and others. With this help, the Federal Military Government managed to muster 85,000 soldiers to wrest back control of Biafran oil from an ill-equipped southern volunteer army. For Britain, however, it was clear that the oil fields of Biafra must be under a stable government to protect their assets. "Our direct interests are trade and investment, including an important stake by Shell/BP in the eastern Region. There are nearly 20,000 British nationals in Nigeria, for whose welfare we are of course specially concerned," notes a declassified Foreign Office memo of the time. That the 20,000 British nationals living in Nigeria are an afterthought to the oil assets which British companies stood to lose from Biafran secession shows just how intrinsically linked oil was to the civil war.

Commonwealth Minister George Thomas wrote another memo in August 1967: "The sole immediate British interest in Nigeria is that ... we can regain access to important oil installations. We cannot expect that economic cooperation between the component parts of what was Nigeria, particularly between the East and the West, will necessarily enable development and trade to proceed at the same level as they would have done in a unified Nigeria; nor can we now count on the Shell/BP oil concession being regained on the same terms as in the past if the East and the mid-West assume full control of their own economies."[52]

Biafran ruler Odumegwu Ojukwu asked Shell and BP for royalties to be paid to his government, rather than the northern Federal one. They refused, and Shell were kicked out of Biafra. The British High Commissioner reported to London that "the only way of preserving unity of Nigeria is to remove Ojukwu by force." Publicly, Britain dutifully supplied small arms and a military flotilla to the Federal Military Government, though stressed that it was for defence, and not to mount an invasion of Biafra and reannexation. Privately, they donated 15 million rounds of ammunition, 500 submachine guns and 21,000 mortar bombs.

The Civil War began officially on 6 July 1967, and lasted nearly three years. The Federal Military Government regained control of Biafra and its invaluable oil – the proceeds of which helped to rebuild the country, ravaged by its internal conflict – in January 1970. At the conclusion of the conflict President Gowon struck a positive tone in his speech; one that, with the benefit of hindsight we now know to be misplaced. "The tragic chapter of violence is just ended. We are at the dawn of national reconciliation. Once again we have an opportunity to build a new nation. My dear compatriots, we must pay homage to the fallen, to the heroes who have made the supreme sacrifice that we may be able to build a nation, great in justice, fair trade, and industry," he said.

Buildings and roads were rebuilt with oil money, patching over the deep cracks that had been there for years and which became enormous fissures under civil war. However the personal and cultural aftermath of the conflict – the three million dead, the mistrust of Britain's private support of the north, and the restoration of oil revenue to the Federal government, with the in-built mistrust that was on both sides – has lasted to today, and is responsible for much of the ill will on both sides of the current Nigerian conflict.

MEND see the Biafran model as something to build upon and improve; an idealised goal of oil independence and fair distribution of revenue, away from international interest. The government see in MEND a dangerous splinter group looking to secede and turn inwards, taking away the prime source of income for the country as a whole. Both sides remember the three million dead, the looming horror of violence, and the starvation. But worryingly both sides believe now, as both sides did then, that the potential spoils of war – all that oil and gas – are worth the bloodshed.

*   *   *

The treatment of one single man has soured relationships between Africa and the west almost irreparably: Ken Saro-Wiwa.

Kenule Beeson Saro-Wiwa (Ken to his friends – and he had many) was born in 1941 in the Niger Delta, home of some of the most rapacious oil and gas drilling that the continent – never mind the nation of Nigeria – has seen from foreign companies. Saro-Wiwa was a staunch supporter during the bloody Nigerian Civil War of the Federal Military Government, believing that the Biafran secession cause was a blow to the whole of Nigeria because of the loss of revenue that would come from the state-within-a-state cutting out on its own. He worked during his life variously as a Civilian Administrator for the port of Bonny (current site of the Bonny LNG plant), the producer of a satirical soap opera, novelist and journalist.

Saro-Wiwa alternated between working for the state and his own independent enterprises; almost everything he seemed to set his mind to, whether teaching, writing or real estate (he was for a short period in the 1970s the owner of a number of real estate and retail businesses), he managed to make work. In essence, Saro-Wiwa was the sort of intellectual mind that most colonists thought simply did not exist in a third world continent such as Africa.

Approaching his 50th birthday, Saro-Wiwa turned his mind towards activism, focusing on human rights and environmental issues in his native Niger Delta. He joined the non-violent Movement for the Survival of the Ogoni People (MOSOP) when the group was still a fledgling campaign organisation, looking to protect their tribal way of life, their environment and their rights to any profits from the oil and gas discoveries made on their land.

At the time Shell were busy producing oil in the Ogoniland, a section of the Niger Delta. Saro-Wiwa, as an eminent local thinker and official spokesman for the MOSOP, claimed that Shell were caught in an endemic circle of ravaging Delta land for oil production, sucking all assets out of the fields below ground then dumping hazardous and toxic petroleum waste in the Delta, seriously harming local wildlife, flora and fauna. The charges laid at Shell were that they had forced their way into the tribe's land and disrupted their idiosyncratic way of life permanently, and the MOSOP were looking for damages. As Anthony Daniels wrote in *The New Criterion*[53], recounting his meeting with Saro-Wiwa: "'The rascals, the rascals!,' Saro-Wiwa exclaimed, and shook the room again with his laughter. *Rascal* is a word that is generally used with a degree of affection, so what Saro-Wiwa said next was all the more shocking. 'They'll kill me, you know. They'll kill me.'"

Saro-Wiwa was eerily prescient. The Nigerian government at the time was constructed of military elites and found the activism, peaceful though it was, troubling. While the Ogoni people in the Niger Delta may not have profited from Shell's drilling, central government certainly was, and was seemingly willing to turn a blind eye to the environmental damage being caused by it. Saro-Wiwa was taken and imprisoned by the government without trial in 1992.

Almost immediately after his release in late 1992, Saro-Wiwa launched a series of marches around Ogoni land. The marches, held in January 1993, attracted crowds of 300,000 – significantly more than half of the whole Ogoni population resident in Nigeria at the time. Saro-Wiwa's cause and campaign was thrust into the international media spotlight, resulting in another month-long jail term for him in June 1993. Almost a year later four Ogoni chiefs were murdered under suspicious circumstances. While Saro-Wiwa was nowhere near the site of the murders (and in fact had been denied access to Ogoniland by Nigerian authorities on the day of them), he was swiftly arrested for incitement to murder. Authorities claimed that during a MOSOP rally on 21 May 1994 Saro-Wiwa had ordered a gang of youths to kill the four chiefs, who were on the more conservative wing of the movement. They produced witnesses to testify that Saro-Wiwa had rallied the youths to murder, most of whom later rescinded their claims, admitting they had been offered lifetime jobs with Shell and bribed with money for their testimony.

"Colleagues the world over believe the charges have been fabricated,"[54] wrote a group of PEN American Center members, including names such as Harold Pinter, Susan Sontag and Chinua Achebe, himself from the Niger Delta, to *The New York Review of Books*, "to silence Mr. Saro-Wiwa who for years has campaigned to secure basic rights for the Ogoni people.

"PEN deplores reports that upon his arrest, Saro-Wiwa was held in shackles in a military prison and was badly beaten on several occasions. His trial, which we fear may not meet the standards established by international law, was scheduled to begin first on January 16 and then on February 6 [1995] but was postponed each time at the prosecution's request. Special tribunals have been condemned as grossly unfair by human rights organizations.

"PEN also objects to the tactics used by security officers guarding the courthouse where Saro-Wiwa is being tried. At the start of the trial on February 21, military guards blocking access to the court building reportedly allowed entry to an observer from the International Commission of Jurists and to another from Shell Oil Company but impeded access to correspondents from the British Broadcasting Corporation and the opposition press. In addition, unconfirmed reports claim that when defense lawyers objected to the military's heavy-handed screening policy, military personnel assaulted them. While PEN welcomes the presence of an envoy from Shell, we urge the government to ensure that the proceedings be open to members of the press and nongovernmental organizations.

"In the absence of any evidence to the contrary, we in PEN believe that Ken Saro-Wiwa has been arrested solely for his work with the MOSOP, including his articles critical of the

Nigerian government's environmental policies in Ogoniland and its treatment of the Ogoni people."

In reality the MOSOP youths were raised to a fury by the fact that Saro-Wiwa was not allowed to attend the meeting by the authorities, not because he had incited them to violence. Nevertheless, Saro-Wiwa was imprisoned with 14 others on the charges.

General Sani Abacha had previously tried to silence Saro-Wiwa by offering him a job in the government as Oil Minister and having been rebuffed, turned viciously on his Civil War ally. So false were the allegations, and so farcical the court proceedings, that almost immediately most of the lawyers working for the defence resigned in protest. Without a prepared defence case, and to the surprise of no-one, Saro-Wiwa and eight other defendants were found guilty. What was shocking to international observers, however, was the harsh response of the courts. Rather than prison sentences, the group soon to be known as the Ogoni Nine were sentenced at the start of November 1995 to death by hanging. Within ten days all nine were hanged, with Saro-Wiwa the last to die, being forced to watch his eight compatriots killed at the hands of the government. Nigeria was immediately suspended from the Commonwealth for its under- and heavy-handed treatment of the MOSOP defendants; then-British Prime Minister John Major called the action "judicial murder." Rumours still abound in the country that General Abacha, then-President of Nigeria, had Saro-Wiwa's hanging videotaped as a memento of the elimination of his foe.

Ill will from the government sanctioned murder of Saro-Wiwa still remains in the Niger Delta today, resulting in the violent (rather than non-violent) resistance of today's groups such as MEND. A suspicion of western international oil companies, thanks to Saro-Wiwa's death stemming from his opposition to Shell's practices in the region, also still holds strong in the region. Their inaction during the trial process – and their paying of \$15.5 million[55] to the families of the victims in supposed hush money days before a trial raised by Saro-Wiwa's son was meant to be brought before a New York court – has left a bad taste with many, and a distrust of the west in general.

* * *

The threat of violence towards oil field workers is not just restricted to those working *on*, but also *near* the lucrative and resource-buoyant Niger Delta. Anglo-French oil and gas driller Perenco faced tragedy and terror in November 2010 – the same month as MEND terrorised Nigeria with multiple kidnappings – when two civilian security contractors employed to defend its Moudi floating storage and offloading (FSO) unit offshore Cameroon were killed. Three soldiers from Cameroon's Batallion d'Intervention Rapide (BIR) were also shot dead in the firefight that resulted from the skirmish. Moudi is very close to the maritime border with Nigeria, and more specifically the Niger Delta. While Nigerian militants did not claim responsibility for the attack on a transport vessel ferrying workers to the oil platform, the proximity to the Niger Delta means that amongst many there was a suspicion of MEND complicity.

Parts of the southeastern Niger Delta were long disputed by Cameroon to be part of their territory, resulting in a protracted argument over the resource-rich swampland that was eventually resolved by Nigeria handing over a section of the land. The International Court of Justice declared the Bakassi peninsula, which juts out into the Gulf of Guinea, as Cameroonian acreage in 2002, but the Nigerian government fought to keep the land for five years before eventually relinquishing the territory – under duress – in August 2008. Since then Nigerian guerrilla attacks, if not orchestrated then possibly tolerated by the Nigerian government, have blighted Cameroonian endeavours in the area.

Government and Niger Delta residents, including organisations such as MEND, were unhappy at international law intruding on a regional matter, removing from their power a land that is believed to have plentiful oil and gas reserves. Additionally the reconfiguring of Bakassi from Nigerian to Cameroonian control meant that many native Nigerians were displaced from their homes on the Delta, causing great upset to residents.

Like many problems that blight the subcontinent, the Bakassi territorial dispute was of colonial making. Queen Victoria signed a Treaty of Protection around the town of Calabar, putting it under the control of the Nigerian Republic (and therefore the British). Prior to this, the Bakassi peninsula had not come under formal border controls of any kind. In fact, the British neglected, in making Bakassi a protectorate, to create a formal border. This proved problematic when the Cameroonians hit back in the middle of the 20th century with documents of their own which showed that Britain had negotiated with the Germans in 1913 (when Germany was looking to take advantage of the shrimping opportunities in the Bakassi area) to give them the Bakassi peninsula in exchange for safe passage to Calabar.

The Bakassi were passed back and forth between British Nigeria and German Kamerun (later British Cameroon when World War II forced Britain to make moves on German colonies in Africa as part of its routing of the Third Reich). That France also entered Cameroon, and that at different points since Queen Victoria signed the Calabar Treaty of Protection in 1884 each country had created legal documents and maps placing the disputed Bakassi area in both Nigeria and Cameroon means that even today, despite the 2002 International Court of Justice declaration, many Nigerians believe Bakassi is Nigerian land, via a tumultuous history as a French or British colony.

It is important to note that though the conflict over the Bakassi territory is between Cameroon and Nigeria, as is the race for oil, the antagonist for both sides is clear. Past colonial masters, in forcing the tribal communities of the Bakassi into a collective country – and then fudging the legal groundwork over its borders – have caused the years of problems around who has the right to Bakassi. That the area may have plentiful natural resources sparked what was already a pressing flashpoint over territory into one over financial gain, and with that added an extra layer of importance to the territorial dispute.

Nigeria would be keen to see the Bakassi return to them because it potentially delivers them another large area of land under which are vast potential resources of oil and gas. Energy is and almost always has been the lifeblood of the Nigerian economy, delivering 95% of export earnings and 65% of total government revenue, according to the Energy Information Administration (EIA)[56]. With reserves the largest in Africa, Nigeria should be at the vanguard of African development. However, as has been seen above with allegations of corruption, the inability to pass into law an effective Petroleum Investment Bill and the constant thorn in the side of government in the shape of MEND, it is lagging behind its potential and is endemic of the struggles African countries are dealing with in order to try and catch up with what we call the 'first world'.

It is, however, the forerunner in Africa. Cameroon has built up 3,000 boundary pillars to prevent Nigeria encroaching on their land. A minority of Bakassi still remaining in what is now Cameroonian land class themselves as Nigerian despite the official transfer of nationality. There is generally a suspicion in Cameroon that despite Nigeria helping its neighbouring country in some industries, there is a soft takeover of the country occurring in an attempt to build a mini African empire under the Nigerian flag. Their fears are not necessarily unfounded: Nigerian Pentecostal pastors are moving into Cameroon in an attempt to spread their religion and 'offering miracles' to gullible locals. In the desire to grasp the land which hold so much potential future earnings, even religion is being commoditised.

This is the problem inherent in working under western, arbitrary boundaries drawn on a map rather than tribal connections. Invariably people get lost when they are forced to act under our western system of strict delineation between countries, and become neighbours with totally different tribes that normally would be ethnically, spiritually and mentally diverse. Stephen Fry related a story typical of the gulf between African and western thinking: upon meeting the President of Uganda, he asked the President which tribe he belonged to. The President dutifully answered, then asked a question which stumped Fry: "and what tribe are you?"[57]

There is such a wide gulf between the perceptions of each culture that it is very difficult to find common cultural ground on which to build understanding. For all that we find Africa's tribal system and crooked young democracies strange (theorists use the concept of 'the Other' to describe it), so they find our non-tribal, relentlessly capitalist society strange. To them, a society built on national, rather than tribal, allegiances, is as perverse as any problems we find their system. The difference is that forced by decades, if not centuries, of being the weaker partner (and often not even being granted the luxury of partner status), they have learnt to compromise and adapt to the western way of conducting business; oftentimes it is a bastardisation of our way, filled with corrupt leaders and laws written more in doggerel than proper prose. Increasingly, however (and despite of the shortcomings which come from such inauspicious beginnings under the colonial yoke), Africa is gaining power and leverage in the world, and their burgeoning democracies and vast wealth of resources give them bargaining chips that did not exist when they were colonies or dominions.

Meeting Africa halfway is the answer that has so long been obvious but overlooked. No longer can foreign oil companies run roughshod over the continent like 21st century imperialists: they must accept the African nations they enter into negotiations with as equal, rather than junior partners, and must share the profits equally. They must promote cultural and regional development, and show that they are not simply interested in the commodity, rather than the people and the future wellbeing of the area. Tribes place great importance on the ground that they live on: to them it is often the source of their food and health. To commoditise that land is an alien concept that they are only just coming to terms with, and as such any negotiations around oil or gas producing areas must be treated carefully and with this past in mind.

There are still problems inherent in this approach, especially in a country such as Nigeria where the thinking of the people and the government seem to be so separate. Who do you answer to when the government does not represent the interests of the people? To foster too close a relationship with government risks alienating the people – a chance which especially in Nigeria, with its violent and organised opposition to drilling, seems too risky to take. However many countries in Africa now find themselves being able to claim correctly that they are a democracy, and in a democracy decisions are taken by the executive branches. Much as a policy of moderation must be the way forward when it comes to neither instilling a western diktat on government nor leaving a country that is comparatively inexperienced in negotiations well alone to founder and fail, a policy of moderation in approaching the people and the government must be used. Without the blessing of government, the licences to drill across Nigeria are unobtainable. Without the blessing of the people, the gas and oil itself is unobtainable. Nigerians are painfully aware of their problems in leadership and infrastructure: "whenever two Nigerians meet," Chinua Achebe wrote in his treatise 'The trouble with Nigeria', "their conversation will sooner or later slide into a litany of our national deficiencies. *The trouble with Nigeria* has become the subject of our small talk in much the same way as the weather is for the English." Because of deficiencies, for example, in the national power infrastructure, the Nigeria Liquefied Natural Gas Plant in River State experienced power cuts which totally wiped out production in the final week of 2010. Sheepishly an official at Bonny LNG told reporters that the simple power outage cost the Nigerian government $60 million in lost revenue[58] from LNG cargoes that would have been exported to Europe at exactly the same period as the west were buckling under the pressure of an extremely cold winter. Achebe's Nigerians are, he goes on, aware that "the vast human and material wealth which she is endowed bestows on her a role in Africa and the world which no one else can assume or fulfill." The people, moreso than the politicians, are aware of Nigeria's standing in Africa as a bellwether of how to deal with the transition from colonial subject to independent democracy – they know they are the litmus test because of their size and comparative maturity as an ostensible democratic, global economy. They are equally aware that there have been significant failings and embarrassments in their recent past which have acted as cautionary examples to others – and they want to ensure that they are spared any future embarrassment.

In such a comparatively unstable country such as Nigeria (which has a torrid history of overthrowing governments at will) gaining the goodwill of the people is almost more important than greasing the pockets of its often-corrupt leaders. They, after all, have the ultimate power in any democracy, whether truly open and free or only partly so: they have the power of the vote.

The simplistic way of looking at Nigeria's problems would be to sum up the entire pre-, post- and colonial history of the nation in a two word phrase: resource curse. Some of the finest economic minds subscribe to the resource curse being an actual event; it may well be, but as has been explored above, it is not the case for Nigeria. Conflict over oil and gas has had an effect, undoubtedly, but it has only exacerbated pre-existing divides between tribes and problems in government with corruption and inaction, rather than caused them.

The problem of managing the expectations and the acceptance of the populace is not only existent in the so-called 'third world', either. International oil and gas companies have long managed to misstep over existing problems and worsen the situation in other areas. In the last decade, companies have faced the ire of locals in County Mayo in north west Ireland over a series of mistakes and attempts to steamroll through plans for an onshore pipeline bringing reserves from the Corrib field to the mainland. In one rural community workers for the producers inadvertently dug up a *cillin* or burial ground for unbaptised babies whose whereabouts was known to the local community but not marked on maps.[59] In a highly conservative Catholic community, this set back relations tremendously, as much as exploiting the Niger Delta and leaving it a wasteland of drilling by-products does in Africa.

In the colonial era the ethnic tribes that line the Niger Delta were just as aware as they are today of the difference between the ordinary people and those in power. Today the influx of money from resources has compounded the gap between want and plenty. Most outrageously a highly-respected Nigerian politician told a member of the US embassy in Lagos that "the Federal Government has not funded one road in the key Niger Delta states in the last ten years."[60] In 2002 several hundred local Delta women had enough of the enormous culture and class gap. They took a boat across a quiet creek which separated the shanty towns from the ChevronTexaco terminal and held a peaceful protest in the oil company's base. 33-year old Roli Ododoh, tending to her two children, told *The New York Times* reporter Norimitsu Onishi after the occupation that "the Bible describes paradise as a beautiful place where there is everything. When we got in there, it was really like paradise."[61]

Corruption and influence in Africa

"The United States must get back into Enugu and Port Harcourt. 'No presence means no access, which leads to no influence. Without influence you have nothing.'"

– US Embassy Cable, 23 February 2010: Assistant Secretary Carson meets oil companies in Lagos

The same cable that gives this chapter its epigraph also explains the problem with Nigeria's gas and oil industry, which can be extrapolated to the rest of Africa's difficulties. "Amateur technocrats run the oil and gas sector according to Shell's Peter Robinson. They believe that they can control the industry via spreadsheets and pushing through the PIB. There are many emotional issues in the PIB with Nigerian politicians believing that they make no money on deep-water projects. Potential banker and businessmen partners do not understand the industry."[62]

Confusion is rife then, and the "emotional issues" and personal interest that can gain large sums of money mean that often unsuitable but entrepreneurial Africans are at the heads of the oil and gas sectors in countries. Corruption therefore opens the way for unscrupulous attempts to gain influence, with companies tempted to take advantage of the naivety of African governments when it comes to hydrocarbon exploitation. Nations look for advice in how to deal with their new natural blessings, and resultantly how to model their often tribal economies on western democratic and homogenised ones in an attempt to replicate their success. What often happens, however, is that friendly advice turns into outright influence and, as Johnnie Carson explained in the leaked US Embassy cable of 23 February 2010, influence leads to the sometimes anticompetitive winning of exploration and production contracts on fields, resulting in increased revenue and a guaranteed supply source from the continent.

Worryingly for the predominately western former colonial powers, African governments are shunning the advice of the western-based international companies, non-governmental organisations and governmental representations in favour of those from Asia. They have seen the same data that the whole world has, and recognised that currently the East is the engine of growth. China, with its expanding economy and its near 1 million barrels of oil per day demand[63] is at the forefront of Asia's representation in Africa, involving itself with trade-in-goods on the continent beyond simply oil and natural gas. Chinese trade with Africa – working in both directions between the continent and the country – rose 43.5% on 2009's figures in the 11 months to December 2010, with a total trade volume value of $114.81 billion.[64] This level of interest in the continent is enormous – but unsettling. Some believe that China is purely self-motivated and is more likely than the west to replay the colonial history which has so blighted Africa in the past. Carson has serious concerns about the eastern power's growing sphere of influence amongst African countries, not least for the future security of the west's hydrocarbon supplies.

"China is a very aggressive and pernicious economic competitor with no morals. China is not in Africa for altruistic reasons. China is in Africa for China primarily. Chinese authoritarian capitalism is politically challenging. The Chinese are dealing with the [Robert] Mugabe's and [Sudanese leader Omar al-] Bashir's of the world, which is a contrarian political model," said Carson to representatives of Shell, Chevron and ExxonMobil at a meeting in his embassy office. The Asian economies are aggressively courting African governments to gain access to their hydrocarbon fields through the highest-possible level of representation: President Hu Jintao has visited more than 20 African nations[65] since he came to power in March 2003.

Corruption is still rife in Africa, and the general populace are more than aware of it.[66] 76% of those questioned in Africa for Transparency International's Global Corruption Barometer said that corruption has either proved intractable or got worse in 2010; more than half the respondents in sub-Saharan Africa paid a bribe of some form or other in the twelve months surveyed. Bribery and corruption are then the norm across all levels of Africa, from large bungs by oil and gas companies to gain easier access to natural resources, to the citizen paying a pittance to an overzealous policeman who has invented a speeding ticket. In

Ghana 74% believe corruption has increased; in Nigeria 83%. Little is being done about corruption either. Only 46% of Nigerians believe their government are making 'effective' efforts to fight corruption; 44% of all sub-Saharan Africans believe efforts have been effective, while 45% believe there has been an ineffective response.

Asked to rate their political parties' corruption on a scale of 1 to 5 (where 5 is extremely corrupt), Nigerians rated their political parties of all hues at 4.5. Quizzed specifically on their government, their responses averaged 4.2. One thing that all of sub-Saharan Africa can agree on is the belief (as explored in the previous chapter) that people power can overcome corruption. 80% believe ordinary people can make a difference in the fight against corruption. Grass-roots movements and personal protests can, as evidenced by the opposition of MEND and ordinary Niger Delta residents to foreign drilling on their land, slow down international oil and gas production significantly. Africans hope that the ability to hold sway over drilling companies can extend to their future need to brook no corruption in the corridors of power. If nothing else (and their actions must be condemned by any right-thinking human) the successes of the likes of MEND in disrupting production in the Niger Delta have shown ordinary people – and international oil companies – that the opinions of the people must be heard, and anyone looking to invest in the Niger Delta especially (and the whole of Africa generally) must now be more cognisant of the will of the people. Influence on the ground is slowly but surely lying more with the people than the politicians.

Influence most of all still remains with the drilling companies, foreshadowing a worrying inability to shake off the colonial shackles of omnipotent western rulers. The US Embassy uncovered how Shell had secreted staff over several years of drilling into the Nigerian government in order to spy on and unduly influence the Nigerian government, by getting wind of and counteracting its next moves. The leaked cables reveal that

Ann Pickard, then Shell's sub-Saharan Vice President, bragged she knew "everything that was being done" in government, including how the country was trying to move away from US dependence by soliciting approaches from China. Ben Amunwa of Platform, an independent overseer and action group for the oil industry, has said that "Shell works deep inside the [Nigerian political] system, and has long exploited political channels in Nigeria to its own advantage."[67]

Pickard met US Ambassador Robin Sanders at the US Embassy in Abuja in late January 2009 to update the government on the situation. She said that "there are some 'very interesting' people lifting oil" in Nigeria.[68] These "very interesting" people included, Pickard went on to say, President Yar'Adua, his wife, Turai and Chief Economic Adviser Tanimu Yakubu, all three of whom, she claimed, accepted bribes for access to oil.

Why does Africa seem to be more corrupt than the west? The problem lies – as most of Africa's problems do – in its colonial past. Ali Mazrui, director of the Institute of Global Cultural Studies wrote on the 50th anniversary of many African nations' independence in December 2010 of the deep schism that the continent has been left with thanks to its former colonial masters.

> Some African historians believe that, despite its relative brevity, the impact of colonialism on Africa has been of epic proportions, deep and wide-ranging. The artificial boundaries of African colonies have made it hard to integrate the populations into real nations. Sub-Saharan Africa continues to be haunted by perennial ethnic rivalries, while Arab Africa has suffered from periodic conflicts between Islam and secularism.
>
> Postcolonial African economies have suffered from shortages of skills and an

abundance of corruption. Three codes of conduct (indigenous, Islamic and western) have created moral incoherence, at least for the time being. [...]

What are the signs for the next 50 years of postcolonial Africa? Most of the continent is still in a pre-democracy era, and many elections are notoriously rigged. However, most African countries stand a good chance of becoming democratised. The real test is when an incumbent president or political party allows itself to be peacefully voted out of office – not once, but at least twice, which led sub-Saharan Africa in the attainment of independence in 1957, has satisfied that condition. [...]

Can Christianity and Islam, both growing in influence across Africa, co-exist peacefully? In reality Christianity and Islam are divisive in Africa if they reinforce prior linguistic and ethnic divisions. Nigeria, for example, has the largest number of Muslims in Africa: almost all its Hausa population are Muslims, almost all its Igbo are Christians, and the Yoruba are split in the middle. Thus Islam reinforces Hausa identity; Christianity reinforces Igbo identity; and Yoruba nationalism unites its people regardless of religion.[69]

That Africa is still struggling under these problems (political instability, corruption, arguments over arbitrary national boundaries, ethnic and religious conflict, and most pressingly for wealth corruption and lack of influence, an absence of a single cohesive moral code) is problematic for the future of the continent. Until these problems are nullified, corruption and the ability to easily influence its leaders in government will remain.

An identity crisis is being used by those expedient enough to take advantage of Africa's shortcomings as an excuse to take without regret some of the continent's most promising assets. In Ghana, detailed below, the government are resisting the lure of rapid development from international companies in favour of slower, more sustainable development. Rather than rushing headlong into unknown territory, they are choosing to try and deal with some of the many problems Mazrui identifies. Already they are the single shining example of a smooth and peaceful transition of power from one democratically elected-government to another; they are aiming to remove corruption and harmful outside influence from their country in favour of helpful but not intrusive international aid; and are trying to create a single moral code of conduct with which to conduct not only business, but everyday life.

Ghana, sadly, is the exception, rather than the rule. In the rapid race – Nigeria's Minister of Petroleum Resources Diezani Alison-Madueke described her country's development as "very aggressive"[70] – to develop infrastructure akin to that of the west (in the hope that doing so will make them more pleasing to western potential partners) African governments and organisations associated with its hydrocarbon resources are overlooking key basic elements that would help mitigate against corruption and losing influence over its own destiny. Here, more than anywhere else in the world, is the often-overused phrase 'learning to run before you can walk' more pertinent. Angola, Equatorial Guinea and Nigeria have been the focus of numerous anti-corruption investigations, including a February 2010 US Senate cross-party investigation into elements of corruption that leaked onto American shores from Africa. All three cases involving the African countries included government contacts, showing that corruption is not simply occurring at low levels.

Government corruption can be the most harmful for the future development of a country, and in Equatorial Guinea and Angola – two countries delved deeper into later in this book that

69

are de facto dictatorships – gaining influence at the highest levels is by the very definition of a dictatorial political system the quickest and most effective way to gain access to hydrocarbon reserves. However in Nigeria, where government has proved ineffective and more than ever access to gas and oil is being controlled (and restricted) by militant groups, Shell's approach of placing observers and agents in government ministries is looking misguided. Rather it is better for companies to follow the power as dictated by public opinion – which would indicate that as readily as companies are willing to engage with and influence government officials, they should equally try to open up lines of conversation with the general populace and its folk leaders, such as the heads of MEND's militants.

That is, of course, easier said than done. As explored above, MEND (and other splinter groups in the oil-rich Delta) are less a controlled group with a strict management structure and more a loose collective of criminals gathered under a single name for convenience. It is difficult to establish whether half the members that claim to be associated with the Movement talk to each other, never mind whether they would talk to foreigners. During the course of writing and researching this book the author tried constantly to question MEND about their organisational makeup, their goals and their tactics. Aside from having difficulty finding contact details for the professed media honcho Jomo Gbomo, a series of emails were sent and remained unreplied to at the time of publication. Infiltrating the criminal gangs that hold the true power in the Niger Delta is almost as difficult as protecting the international workers on the drilling platforms in the labyrinthine and unwelcoming Niger Delta itself.

Even if companies were able to secrete insiders with governments or militants, would (predominately western) companies feel comfortable doing so? The evidence indicates that frankly they are, though whether this is from a necessity and recognition that simply this is the way things are done in

Africa or a more proactively willing stance is unknown. Undoubtedly doing so draws unfavourable responses in the west – and from the African public too. One need only look at the sullied standing of Shell in Nigeria for most of its time in the country, and the two flashpoints of unfavourable media coverage in the west (at Shell's inaction in the Ken Saro-Wiwa case and the Wikileaks cables revelations of control over government) to see that it is a dangerous public relations game. Yet it happens, because it is the only way to keep ahead, and often it is the only way to get things done in Africa in its current make-up.

There is though a wish that Africa can grow out of its corrupt practices which is professed by African hoi polloi, officials, international oil and gas companies, governments and NGOs alike. The sticking point is that to do that there must be an incentive to move away from the idea that corrupt politicians can be open to influence in negotiating contracts or allowing access to key officials or data for the right price. Currently just offering an alternative, rather than keenly disincentivising those who are willing to be corrupt, would likely go a long way. Wholesale shying away from corrupt practices on the behalf of international drillers is needed – but the rising spectre of China and India (two countries known for their dexterity in bending the rules when it comes to corruption and undue influence) indicates that is unlikely to happen.

In Africa there is a will, but maybe not a way out of corruption – at least not right now. "Africa is not always an easy place to do business", Dino Mahtani laconically wrote in *The Financial Times*.[71] Corruption has become so commonplace in African countries, and in the hydrocarbon sectors of those countries specifically – that it is even able to take hold before a country produces first oil.

Uganda had yet to produce their first gas or oil in enough volume to sell internationally before their government officials – including Mineral Development Minister Hilary Onek – were offered bribes for implicit and explicit support of Italian oil giant Eni's bid to take exploration and production rights from Heritage Oil. The Wikileaked US diplomatic cable sent in December 2009 from its embassy in Kampala to Washington declared that "this is a critical moment for Uganda's nascent oil sector [which will] have profound consequences for transparency and openness in the future management of the industry."[72]

Tullow Oil, an Irish company which owes a large amount of its fame and success today to spotting early on the future potential of Africa, owned (and still own) a raft of acreage over several exploration blocks in Uganda, with more than 9,000km² of land proven to contain oil and gas reserves, as well as swathes of other exploration sites which hold promise for future reserves. Less than two weeks before Christmas in 2009 Tullow's Regional Vice President for Africa Tim O'Hanlon met the US' Ugandan Ambassador Jerry Lanier, a career diplomat who had solved crises in Korea, Afghanistan, Pakistan and Bangladesh before settling in Africa for a gentle retirement. The US embassy in Kampala was festooned with Christmas decorations, but O'Hanlon was not in a festive mood. While Tullow were punching above their financial weight in exploring and finding producing blocks in Uganda and other African countries – and struggling to sell them on to larger companies (including China's CNOOC, Total SA and ExxonMobil, to all of whom Tullow were offering minority shares in blocks 1, 2 and 3A) with the financial clout to extract the oil by finding them through legal tendering – Heritage Oil were trying to sell their exploration and production licences to Eni through "a corrupt back door deal." Ministers unrelated to the energy sector were coming out in public and backing Eni's claims to invest in the country – and Mineral Minister Onek had "grandstanded" (to use O'Hanlon's own words) in the Ugandan parliament, crowing over Eni's suitability and treating the whole situation as if it was a done deal. O'Hanlon wanted to use his recourse to the British High Commission and the US Ambassador to help shine a light on the corruption and ensure that the potential canker worm of corruption did not get hold of another African nation, or else he would use his company's rights to pre-empt the sale and regain total control of the blocks. In the end Tullow bought out Heritage's shares in the blocks for $1.5 billion, though without the prior approval of the Ugandan government, meaning that Tullow and the Ugandan government have since been frosty in relations with each other as they jostle over a $404 million unpaid tax bill relating to the Heritage deal. O'Hanlon was forced to write a letter to President Museveni of Uganda dated 10 December 2010 dialling back the criticisms of government officials:

His Excellency,

Yoweri Kaguta Museveni

President of the Republic of Uganda

State House

Entebbe

Uganda

10th December 2010

No doubt you have been made aware of the illegal theft of confidential communications from various US Embassies around the world including that in Kampala and the publication of selected and often doctored elements of these on the internet.

In one such release, I have been mentioned as accusing your Honourable Ministers ONEK and MBABAZI of involvement in corruption during a meeting I had with the US ambassador last year. This is absolutely false.

Of course, I never made such a claim to the US ambassador but merely discussed with him at our meeting in December 2009 the detailed stories published in the previous week's local press and the associated rumours circulating in Kampala at that time. I have no evidence to present implicating the Honourable Ministers in corruption and have no reason to believe that the rumours sweeping Kampala at the time were actually true.

In answer to the many media enquiries which have flooded Tullow since the Wikileaks publication, we have released the following statement to the Press :-

"As part of a general discussion about doing business in Africa with the US ambassador to Uganda, I made reference to a number of rumours then in circulation in the local media in Kampala to illustrate the issues the oil and gas industry faced. At no time did I give any credence to these rumours and would therefore dispute the record of our conversation as detailed by Wikileaks. In fact, President Museveni's government rightly insisted on a transparent process - which led directly to the joint venture agreement between CNOOC, Total and Tullow."

I can assure Your Excellency that we will continue to monitor these matters closely and will work in any way we can with the two Ministers involved to help clear their names. I remain available in Kampala and welcome any advice you may have to offer in this regard and sincerely regret this entire unhappy episode.

Respectfully Yours

Tim O'HANLON

Vice-President, African Business

The letter is an attempt to smooth over the rift caused between Tullow and the government as the company attempts to undo damage caused by the accusations of double-dealing within government. Here in Uganda was a company willing to abide by the rules being wholly outmanoeuvred by a larger exploration and production company who were less moralistic about the concept of corruption in an African state, threatening to strangle the possibility of an uninfluenced, incorrupt society at birth. The problem is that it is far too tempting, and significantly too easy, for officials first tasting the financial spoils of huge reserves to take their own cut in exchange for favouring one international company over the other.

The Ugandan government tried to justify listening to Eni (though not the accepting of the bribes by officials) by saying that Tullow's dominance in the Ugandan market was hampering competition in the sector. There is, of course, a strong and very valid argument that a single-company monopoly on gas and oil assets would allow the Irish company undue influence over the government and the hydrocarbon sector, akin to that which dictatorial leaders exert over countries. African governments then are put into a difficult situation. Such is the standard set by their previous incarnations that the populace and international observers often believe that any closeness between government officials and international companies is automatically a corrupting one aimed at gaining undue influence. They must, though, rely on the expertise of foreign companies to allow them to steadily and carefully grow their hydrocarbon sector, using the knowledge which comes naturally to drilling companies from years of experience around the world but is so often lacking in these young democracies. They also must not, as some, including Director General of the Nigerian Security and Exchange Commission Arunma Oteh believe, rely on oil alone to stimulate and grow their economy. Oteh blamed Nigeria's comparative economic backwardness for a nation which celebrated its fiftieth year of independence on an overreliance and dependence on oil at the expense of diversification of the economy.[73]

A change of tack is needed from both sides. The African people must have more faith in their leaders, and more trust in the benevolence of international companies. The west must likewise think more highly of African leaders and not let the notion that they could be corrupted by bribes or pressured into being influenced alter the way they present their claims to oil and gas fields. For too long the west has viewed Africa as a pushover, a mini-colony of their own upon which they can place their ideals and take their gas and oil for little recompense. The problem is a common one in the postcolonial world: a fear, mistrust and poor perception of the Other half in the relationship. The west views Africa as being too different, and believes imposition of western beliefs and standards is the way to succeed. Africans believe the west are marauding and self-centred, always looking to further their cause in the continent and taking advantage of Africa's nascence. The tired 'third world'/'first world' dichotomy still exists on both sides. The terms 'first world' and 'third world' are not in themselves so bad, but placing them in a prism of ranking is. Implicit in the labelling is a belief that the first world is somehow better or more entitled to success. However that belief in a ranking still exists between the 'first' and 'third' worlds; indeed, it exists within Africa, where larger, more developed countries in the oil and gas sector pull rank and are seen as the domineering older brother to their younger siblings.

Ghana

"There are obvious challenges that confront the oil and gas industry today. There are also present great opportunities. When harnessed properly these opportunities could be transformed into sustainable development for all stakeholders and Ghanaians in particular. Are we prepared for the challenges ahead? Provided we are willing NOT to do it the usual Ghanaian way (good polices, no action), the answer will be 'Yes, we can.'"

– Ghanaian Ministry of Energy, 'The Emerging Oil and Gas Sector'

The BBC's David Amanor has claimed that "the post-colonial relationship [between Nigeria and Ghana] has been characterised by a kind of sibling rivalry".[74] Ghana appreciates the work Nigeria does in the region to keep the peace, but is more than willing to constantly point out that Nigeria meddles in other countries' business while being unable to mind their own borders.

Ghana however is able to learn from Nigeria's mistakes when it comes to handling the vast quantity of natural resources that they sit on. Politically gas is vital to Ghana's future development and their hope of becoming one of Africa's major economies. The nation's press are crowing about the possibilities of gas and oil to change their fortunes via an influx of foreign investment and an unparalleled spate of job creation. As with the example of Nigeria, however, foreign investment in a country does not necessarily equate to an improvement in the fortunes of that country. Nor does the establishment of gas and oil drilling platforms, transmission networks and refineries lead to jobs for Ghanaian nationals in the industry. In this way, Amanor's analogy of the two countries acting as an older and younger sibling proves even more useful for Ghana. It is able to see how Nigeria has been divided by the prospect of revenue from natural gas and oil exploration and ensure that it is more careful than its 'elder sibling' in making sure that the potential profligacy of politicians who see an opportunity to gain from the wealth of natural resources does not occur and split the nation along class lines.

Ironically while Ghana considers Nigeria to be its older brother, it is in fact the former that is the older of the two nations – and was initially the head of a west African empire of its own. The land we know today as Ghana came under the control of the British as a crown colony in 1874 under the name of the Gold Coast. Named after its plentiful resources of the precious metal, the Gold Coast was an exemplar of the resource colonisation that perhaps even moreso than British colonisation of the Indian subcontinent was endemic of the empire. For more than 50 years before it was officially instated as a colony of the crown, the Gold Coast had been under the sway of Britain, who seized land from the natives, from the Dutch, and from the Danes. While the rulers installed western amenities such as railways and hospitals that ultimately proved positive for the country, they also followed the same pattern of taking resources without returning much of the profit to the country it came from, and forced disparate tribes together in a way similar to that in Nigeria and the Cameroon which caused such injurious infighting in later years.

The colonial-era western profiteering from natural resources in the Gold Coast was not as self-interested as in Nigeria; here, a decent (though not fair) proportion of profit was directed back into the community, meaning that today there is less distrust in foreign companies here than in other, more maltreated African nations.

The Gold Coast was the first sub-Saharan African nation to gain independence from its rulers in 1957, taking the name Ghana. Ghanaians are proud of their independence and freedom from western rule, still remembering today the founding motto of the newly-independent Republic of Ghana: "free forever". As with Nigerian President Goodluck Jonathan's choice of clothing reminding the country of its colonial past, so Ghana has a similar – and more permanently totemic – symbolic message. Its flag represents the blood spilt for independence in its top red stripe, its mineral wealth in the middle gold band, and its rich agricultural land in the bottom green stripe. The black star which overlays all three colours is a permanent symbol of Africa's emancipation from colonial rule. Here, as in the rest of Ghana, symbolism (and tradition) rules strongly.

Those founding words "free forever" were spoken by Kwame Nkrumah in 1957, Ghana's first Prime Minister and President. Also prescient in the minds of modern-day Ghanaians was his other founding assertion, that Africa as a whole would not fall into the trap of neo-colonialism, whereby out of custom and comfort the formerly subject countries of an empire or coloniser continue the master-servant arrangement but on a more informal basis.

Neo-colonialism is a real fear for most of Africa, especially with the balance of power in commodities such as gas and oil lying with the former colonial masters. African leaders must carefully tread the line between making the most of their bountiful resources and allowing foreign western investment while making sure that it does not sleepwalk them into a second colonial era. In this manner, negotiations with African countries on the basis of drilling, exploration and production must take care not to give off the impression of meddling nor talking down to potential producing nations. Neither liberal guilt nor right-wing jingoism and superiority (colonial apologies or colonial celebrations) are needed: the political middle ground is a sacred place from which to approach Africa's colonial past - and it coincidentally happens to be the perfect place to hold negotiations over oil and gas rights. Meeting in the middle is so often platitudinally used to describe how to negotiate – in reality it rarely happens, with one side inveighing over the other. Here, it really is the answer.

Ghana has not been an unqualified postcolonial success story, however. Fifteen years of coups and countercoups ended with Flight Lieutenant Jerry Rawlings becoming President of the country in 1981, causing a mass migration of many Ghanaians (with most going to nearby Nigeria). Rawlings suspended political parties and the Ghanaian constitution on taking power and the country only returned to fair party politics in 1992. Rawlings was removed from power through fair elections in 2000, though his former Vice President in the military dictatorship, John Atta Mills, won the 2008 open election with a majority of just less than half a percent for his National Democratic Congress. While the second fair and legitimate transfer of power in the nation's history means that today Ghana is considered a stable democracy, Mills' past as a central part of a military ruling party shows just how rapidly African countries can move from unfair autarchy to fair democracy (and hypothetically, just how quickly they could also move the opposite way).

Many within the country see 2011 as its breakout year as oil production looks set to ramp up significantly. As of 2010 Ghana had proved reserves of nearly 2 billion barrels of oil[75] and 22.65 billion cubic metres (bcm) of gas[76]; its oil production was only about 7,000 barrels a day (of which two-thirds was exported), while it produced no natural gas. Ghanaians have a healthy suspicion of the aims of oil companies; GhanaWeb, a portal for Ghanaians has warned that "oil companies are the most difficult corporate groups to deal with in the extractive industry and it would be disastrous for Ghana if legal framework that is dated, weak and contains gaps is to be used to govern the oil and gas industry. Oil companies have strong incentives to maximize profits and the availability of weak and unenforceable environmental and health laws could lead to gruesome abuse."[77]

It is not just outside observers that viewed the impending oil bubble with wariness: Ghana's Finance Minister Kwabena Duffuor scaled down his production figures for 2011[78] and resultantly the revenue from a high of $1.2 trillion to a more realistic $400 million in his budget. Duffuor based his figures on producing 60,000 barrels a day at a price of $40 a barrel (just over half the actual traded price at the time, and since early 2011 tumult in nations like Tunisia and Egypt, a minority proportion of the now-$100 a barrel price) in an attempt to downplay the potentially massive impact oil revenues could have on the struggling economy. With high inflation and deficits running nearly 20% of GDP, Duffuor would like nothing more than to see an oil boom in his country, but at the risk of overplaying its importance with several key regulatory issues still to be resolved, he erred on the side of caution in presenting his figures to the populace. The International Monetary Fund had no such qualms about downplaying the potential of the country's oil reserves: Ghana could make $20 billion from the commodity by 2030.[79]

Indeed the entire government seems to be taking a gently-gently approach to oil and gas, perhaps because of the chaos they are confronted with day-on-day in nearby Nigeria. Written in the founding aims of the Ghana National Petroleum Company (GNPC), formed in 1985, are undertakings to "ensure that Ghana obtains the greatest possible benefits from the development of its petroleum resources" and "to ensure that petroleum operations are conducted in such a manner as to prevent adverse effects on the environment, resources and people of Ghana." The GNPC oversees the twelve ongoing offshore developments in the country that have been granted licences.

The problem for the GNPC is that Ghana is entering relatively unknown territory in the hydrocarbon sector and has heretofore no knowledge of how to operate. As Chinua Achebe explains of Africa as a whole,

> during the colonial period, struggles were fought, exhaustingly, on so many fronts — for equality, for justice, for freedom — by politicians, intellectuals and common folk alike. At the end of the day, when the liberty was won, we found that we had not sufficiently reckoned with one incredibly important fact: If you take someone who has not really been in charge of himself for 300 years and tell him, "O.K., you are now free," he will not know where to begin. This is how I see the chaos in Africa today and the absence of logic in what we're doing. Africa's postcolonial disposition is the result of a people who have lost the habit of ruling

themselves, forgotten their traditional way of
thinking, embracing and engaging the world
without sufficient preparation.[80]

Ghana's MPs are divided and dithering over how to
muster the country and formulate a single approach to the oil
and gas blessings they have in negotiations with experienced
and canny international potential partners. One wing believes
that Ghana should draw on international drilling companies'
experience in negotiations over hydrocarbons and ask them to
help the government thrash out a fair and useful revenue
management chain; others fear that to do so is to allow Ghana to
be exploited by companies driven by profit, their concerns
fuelled by an all-too sharp awareness of how quickly Ghana fell
into colonialism – and how long it took to battle out of it.

There is caution, then, fuelled by uncertainty. Initial
public celebrations around the first oil and gas discoveries in the
country have been replaced by quiet optimism that is nearly
always tempered by pragmatism. Some are concerned by
government inexperience, and almost every step is overanalysed
by the populace to ensure that it is in the best interests of the
people, meaning that resultantly the government are even more
trepid in their actions.

When the parliament tried in 2010 to scrap a planned
Public Interest and Accountancy Committee (PIAC), set up to
ensure transparency in commodity negotiations because sections
of the Petroleum Revenue Management Bill being legislated at
the time (according to the text of its final draft) already "makes
great effort to respond to the need for accountability and
transparency", the public and Ghanaian media responded with
outrage, believing that it seriously compromised the nascent oil
and gas state sector. One leader article in Ghanaian newspapers
written by Stephen Yeboah[81], a non-governmental organisation
employee said that the scrapping of the committee "is especially
dangerous in the African region where the leader or politician

cannot be trusted for a second. Corruption has registered its feet in the continent and it takes comprehensive provisions of transparency, openness and accountability to bring salvation." This all because of the government wanting to cut down on waste, currently having two separate sections of bureaucracy dealing with the same issue.

Indeed Ghana have gone further than most in assuring western countries, companies and their own people of their transparency. They are one of just two countries in Africa (and five in the world) to be fully compliant with the Extractive Industries Transparency Initiative (EITI), an initiative which compels companies and governments to disclose payments and have them verified by an independent group of observers. Through their overcaution driven by an admitted inexperience, Ghanaian officials have managed to avoid the pitfalls many other African countries fell into in the dash to exploit their resource revenue.

Nigeria – who have so strongly felt the problems of a rush to resources – were the first nation to try to sign up to EITI in 2003, in an attempt to quell the anger of those in the Niger Delta who believed corruption and self-interest were hampering the chances of their region profiting from its oil and gas reserves. As of yet Nigeria have not become an EITI compliant country, but rather are an EITI candidate country, that the group acknowledged in October 2010 are "close to compliance". If all goes well, Nigeria could become an EITI compliant country by March 2011[82], though backing from Transparency Initiative and the World Bank[83] seems unlikely to stop MEND's campaign against the government and international companies.

As part of their EITI declaration Ghana realise they need to form a national oil and gas policy which aims to make the country "a net exporter of oil and gas and a major player in the global petroleum industry, through the development and management of the nation's petroleum resources and revenue streams in a transparent and environmentally responsible manner for the benefit of every Ghanaian, now and in the future"[84] – a similar aim to those of the founding responsibilities of the GNPC. Within the national policy MPs are thrashing out details of both the Petroleum Production & Exploration Bill and the Petroleum Regulatory Authority Bill. While the ultimate goals (including the need to "provide a fair government take as well as an acceptable return for the energy companies", "create conditions that are initially attractive, so that risk capital is provided" and "maximise the development of hydrocarbons to advance economic conditions in [the] country (exploit market chain)") are agreed upon, the minutiae of the bills are yet to be agreed. The government have agreed on the creation of a new National Petroleum Authority that will initially be given rule over the entire industry; the GNPC will be alleviated of its role as de facto regulator and become responsible for exploration licensing, funded in part by a $38 million credit to be paid back over 35 years to the Ghanaian government by the World Bank. Tentativeness in shoring up details of the bills is amplified by the concerns of the people that the hydrocarbon blessing does not become a colonial curse, but an excess of caution has meant that the legislative infrastructure needed is not in place despite the first trickles of oil occurring in the country.

Strangely the fear of neo-colonialism that reverberates loudest in Ghana is not that of British, European or American countries, but Asian ones. Bolstered by being one of the few regions not to suffer the detrimental effects of the economic depression, strident economies in China, Japan, Korea and India have come forward with offers to take stakes in Ghanaian fields that have been applied for on behalf of European investors – and rejected by government. Palms have been greased in a transparent manner by coupling the offers of investment in oil and gas fields to large loans. CNOOC, the China National Offshore Oil Corporation, offered to buy into a 23.5% stake in the Jubilee field and include a $5 billion loan as part of the package. The Chinese Development Bank has previously bankrolled significant parts of the existing oil infrastructure in

Ghana through preferential loans totalling billions of dollars. These are all part of unprecedented international investments from the Chinese: the China Export-Import (Exim) Bank and the Chinese Development Bank handed out loans of at least $110 billion to developing countries from the start of 2009 to the end of 2010; similar arms of the World Bank – a theoretically much larger entity – only handed out a smidgen over $100 billion over a similar timescale.[85] For China, like the colonialists of the late 19th century, "the business of empire, once an adventurous and often individualistic enterprise, ha[s] become the empire of business."[86]

China are able to advance quicker further than its western counterparts in Africa because of twinned circumstances: it has risen just as the western economic bubble collapsed into recession, meaning that it can easily outpurchase any competitors from Europe or the US (who are often kept in liquidity by long-term loans from the Chinese itself, who seem to have a neverending wealth of credit) and it, moreso than the former colonial powers, can claim to better understand the struggles with development. Indeed China could be seen as an example to Africa of how to mediate traditional cultural beliefs and ways of life with the western desire for democracy, having become a hugely successful centre of commerce in a relatively short space of time. David Greely of Goldman Sachs has said "countries that export to China are the ones doing well"[87] in the current market, with China demanding upwards of a million barrels of oil per day, and their growth slowing only slightly (from 10.1% in 2010 to 9.5% in 2012), meaning they will still require 800,000 barrels more oil each year than the last. Other Asian economies that are on the ascendancy (or have risen from similar levels in the more recent past than the west) are also given more careful hearing because of their circumstances.

Japan sent its Crown Prince Naruhito to Ghana in March 2010 to offer to invest in the same stake that China was seeking in Jubilee with a $4 billion loan and $1.5 billion in credit. India have promised in the past few years to install billion-dollar industrial plants across the country under the assumption that the gas needed to fire them would come free or at a highly reduced rate. The ordinary Ghanaians' response to this is clear: one wrote "our dear nation and its politicians shouldn't be greedy as other African countries [are]. They discover the mineral due to greediness [which] allows Caucasians to rip them off – look at Nigeria! [They are] the largest African oil producers and among the world's largest too…do we want to be in the same shambles, all in the name of greedy politicians?" Another was equally clear: "the oil has come to assist us; [it is] for the development and improvement of our motherland. But what is going on at the moment [might] result in divisions and tribal wars if care is not taken." As concerning as the looming threat of local resources being taken by international companies is the vast amounts of voluntary debt that arrangements with the Asian countries would involve incurring. Already Ghanaian MPs have agreed to a bill allowing the government to use up to 70% of all oil and gas revenues as collateral on huge international loans,[88] indicating that they see the incurring of debt as a legitimate method of growing their economy (its 2010 Budget aimed for growth of 12.3% in 2011) and that such a method can be bankrolled by hedging its hydrocarbon revenue as insurance against defaulting on those debts.

Also problematic is that government has little personal impetus to act quickly or fairly. Ghanaian parliamentarians are the lowest paid MPs in Africa[89] – despite an October 2010 pay rise of 17% and the offer of a free laptop to each member in an attempt to improve the quality of their democratic thinking. "The essence was to make it easier for MPs to access information easily in their research work towards building a quality democracy," said deputy leader of the majority Rashid Pelpuo of the perks of the job. Each of Ghana's 230 MPs makes $24,000 a year, including their bursary for allowances. Despite their comparatively low pay when put alongside other African parliamentarians, Ghana's MPs and state officials seem to value integrity and scruples more than most other African nation's representatives: the nation ranked above Russia, Egypt, Mexico and Morocco on Transparency International's 2010 Corruption Perceptions scale, with a cleanliness score of 4.1 out of a possible 10. The average wage for the whole of Ghana, however, is little more than $700, meaning that for many Ghanaians there is still a huge discrepancy between the politicians and the people.

Dr Mohammed Ibn Chambas, Secretary-General of the African, Caribbean and Pacific Countries Council warned that "the government is obliged to do a balancing act with regard to the sharing of oil revenue. In the end both national considerations and the demand[s] of the chiefs and people of the western region need to be addressed." He went on to explain to Ghana's national newspaper The Daily Graphic that gas and oil revenue "should be used to address the infrastructure deficit in the country, as well as improve the quality of life of the people. A lopsided [arrangement] will result in further agitation by some sections of the masses; a situation Ghana is not prepared for in this critical moment of its development."[90]

Government seems to be taking heed of Chambas' (and the population's) warnings. Ghana's Chief Justice, Georgina T Wood has called for an overhaul of the country's university system to align itself more closely with the impending direction the country will take as oil and gas exploration and production becomes its primary industry. "It is time," she told students at a Ghanaian commencement ceremony, "tertiary education considered positioning itself to take opportunities that are uncovered on a daily basis so that Ghanaians can take their destiny into their own hands – especially in the field of oil." A respondent to the PwC Oil & Gas Survey 2010 was quoted as saying "there is [a] need for more local participation in the oil and gas business. We currently have too much dependence on expat(s), both human and technical." Wider responses back this assertion: a third of respondents employ expats in more than half of their senior and middle management positions alone.

While it has been explored above that Finance Minister Kwabena Duffuor had struck a cautionary tone in presenting the 2011 budget to the people, even his conservative estimates still see industrial growth of 25.4% in 2011, an astonishing figure that far outstrips any other sector in Ghana.

Ghana is concerned not to follow Nigeria's hubris when it first gained independence and rushed to have all the trappings of a modern state. General Olusegun Obasanjo, then-President of Nigeria said in his farewell tour with pride that "Nigeria will become one of the ten leading nations in the world by the end of the [20th] century" – a prediction that ultimately fell flat on its face in ignominy. In the race for western 'civilisation' without shoring up the basic infrastructure and moral codes needed, Nigeria has (according to Chinua Achebe) become "one of the most disorderly nations in the world. It is one of the most corrupt, insensitive, inefficient places under the sun[;] dirty, callous, noisy, ostentatious, dishonest and vulgar."

Ghana has, however, fallen into a common trap that most African nations have when it comes to modernisation and westernisation that is typical of the pitfalls that trying to overreach too soon. At the turn of the millennium many nascent African democracies saw the need to gain an online presence, believing it was the done thing for governments in the west to be accountable and accessible to the people over the internet, which has seen a boom in users as Africa begins to be connected via broadband.[91] In 1998 fewer than 6,000 people were connected to the internet in Ghana (0.03% of the population); now more than 1.3 million, or 5%, are online. Nigeria has undergone an even more staggering online revolution, rising from 30,000 users in 1998 to 44 million, or one in every four Nigerians, in 2009. As an indication of how connected Nigeria is, Britain has only 8 million more internet users and Russia 3 million fewer. This personal online renaissance has not translated to government, however. Today many of these websites lie dormant, a frippery forgotten about when it was realised that more pressing needs such as a firm infrastructure were needed to be arranged above luxuries such as websites. Most were last updated more than four or five years ago.

The Volta River Authority (VRA) is one such public sector group in Ghana that is fossilised permanently on the internet as an example of where government moved too soon towards the western model. Established in 1961, the company oversees the generation of electricity for use by all sectors in the country. On its homepage, it claims proudly that it could be "the Ontario of Africa". While some sections of the website are more up-to-date than others (the footer on the site explains it was last updated in February 2010 – still an age away on the internet), the Authority has a section publishing its annual reports – following the lead of total transparency that many similar groups in Europe and the US demonstrate. The last working link is to the 2005 Annual Report; the 2009 report is linked to, but does not work. When this writer contacted the Authority asking to be emailed the 2009 edition, a reply came that an electronic version does not exist – but "in case you are in Accra, kindly come to our office at the Electro-Volta House" to see a hard copy.[92]

In many ways this is indicative of how unprepared Africa is in general for the oil and gas boom that it is on the precipice of. When production was dictated by international oil companies, transparency and public accounting on an international scale was not needed – to the detriment of the people. Now with government taking a more active role in controlling its assets, the transparency is needed, but inexperience of such an approach and a lack of staff trained in the sector means that such things are overlooked. Before the active marketing of gas and oil interests to the international community, the only people who likely would need access to the group's accounts *would* be able to drop into the VRA offices in Accra. Today that is not the case, and patience and an awareness is needed that for all that what the west consider integral parts of infrastructure are missing or deficient, the desire for openness is there. If western investors can acknowledge this, and become more sympathetic to the problems precipitated by Africa's starting position when it comes to open democracy and free economics, then it stands a chance of standing equal to or better than similar Chinese, Japanese, Korean and Indian bids which ultimately will only serve to propagate African subservience.

The one major factor which favourably distinguishes western oil and gas companies from their eastern counterparts is their experience. The largest British, European and American exploration and production companies have been working for more than a century and pump billions of dollars annually into developing their technological prowess further. They are a safe pair of hands with which to trust potentially destiny-altering levels of revenue from hydrocarbon production – as long as they can assure African governments that entering into business with them will provide a fair deal and not a rehash of one-sided colonial practices.

To that end, an awareness of cultural differences between Ghana and the west must be formed. Basic social structures that we in the west take as given, such as patrilineality (where our ancestry is generally traced through paternal relations, including the adopting of a father's surname) are often not repeated in West African tribes such as those living in Ghana. Ghanaian philosopher Kwame Anthony Appiah hinted at difficulties he faced correlating his twin ancestries as a mixed-race child in an interview with Al-Jazeera's Riz Khan: "my father's family is matrilineal – that is, you belong to your mother's family. And my mother is from England, and her family thought you belong to your father's family. Those are two different ways of thinking about family life"[93]. Such fundamental differences in thinking which would ordinarily go unthought of by each side because their view of the world centred around their own society can unwittingly hamper any potential negotiations from the off. The concept that a society could approach something as basic as family lineage in a different way to our own shows how tricky negotiating across the culture gap can be, and the unconscious linking of that to notions of an Other viewpoint (with its similarly unwitting negative associations) works in both directions. To Ghanaians the notion that we take our father's name when we are born is as strange and abnormal as their way is to us. We have in our wholly polarised approaches to something as seemingly basic as this a distinct postcolonial Othering: each side finds the other so different – and inferior – that a superiority complex cannot help but be engendered. At least one nation – China – has acknowledged that Africa's cultural idiosyncrasies must be behoven to. Richard Dowden of the Royal African Society explained that "The Chinese are beginning to realise that since so much of African politics is driven by groups or individuals below the official state level they will have to understand and engage with these dynamics. That means meeting leaders of the opposition, negotiating with local chiefs and kings in areas where the Chinese operate even though they have no status at official national level."[94]

Problematically oil companies operating in the Ghana's Jubilee field, including Tullow Oil have tried to impose foreign policy constraints on the Government of Ghana in conditions contained within the Jubilee Field Unit Crude Oil Lifting Agreement discussed in December 2010.[95] The terms state that "all export tankers owned, technically managed or commercially operated by a company headquartered in, or flying flags of US-sanctioned countries shall be automatically rejected. At present these countries are Cuba, Iran and Sudan", all three of which have invested heavily into the infrastructure of Ghana's education and health system. An opinion piece for the *GhanaWeb* website writes that Tullow's demands – and their reservation of the "right to specify further flag states" to be not negotiated with as per US sanctions – would "turn Ghana into a poodle" of the west, language which harks back to the days of colonialism. A balance must be struck between maintaining the beliefs of the west to follow internationally-mandated sanctions and aligning thought with African countries, who often do not sign up to such groups out of pragmatism. Often countries considered by the west to be rogue states are the most supportive of the developing world because they have been frozen out of the developed world by sanctions (right or wrong) and therefore see Africa as a vital trading partner. For a shipping company to attempt to dictate foreign policy without consideration of Ghana's role as an independent thinking state smacks of a new wave of imperialism to Ghanaian minds.

*　　*　　*

The West African Gas Pipeline (WAGP) restarted flows between Ghana and Nigeria (via Togo and Benin) in April 2010 after a year of lying dormant thanks to vandalism – including some where the suspected culprits were Nigeria's MEND – and problems with sustaining suitable fuel quality. The pipeline initially reached landfall in Ghana in December 2008, but never properly made full use of its capacity due to the various teething problems and attacks. The average flows over the pipeline have never risen above 30 million standard cubic feet (mmscf) a day, and likely never will because of problems with Nigeria being unable to meet its own domestic demand. Indeed, Nigeria has capped its maximum flow to Ghana at 170mmscf/day, a figure which is not enough to meet Ghana's forecast natural gas demand.

This places the imperative on retaining some of the resources that look to be drilled in the country's impending energy boom. For all Ghana will be able to fuel large parts of the world's energy demand through its plentiful oil and gas reserves, if it is not able to provide enough for its own people discontent with government and the international companies taking its oil and gas will rage.

The fear of piracy on a pipeline connected to the militant-dominated country of Nigeria is also at the forefront of the collective minds of the Ghanaian Ministry for Energy. Within a presentation[96] to the Extractive Industries Transparency Initiative (EITI) is a list of possible security threats to the country's hydrocarbon resources. Amongst them include "oil thefts on the high seas by organised criminals" like MEND, "piracy and hostage taking" and "militant locals who may disrupt onshore installations under the pretext of securing more oil wealth for their communities" – all worries for any potential international investors in Ghana's oil and gas industry, especially given the precedent in Nigeria, whose militants have managed to siphon off significant amounts of oil and gas for personal gain, disrupted production, spilt blood and kidnapped then extorted large ransoms from foreign companies.

This is more an overly cautious approach to government and regulation and exploitation of the hydrocarbon sector, however; one which has been recognised by the international community and praised as a prime indicator of Ghana's role as a flagship African democracy. US President Barack Obama spoke to Ghanaian MPs in parliament on 11 July 2009 in his unique professorial cadence:

> Here in Ghana, you show us a face of Africa that is too often overlooked by a world that sees only tragedy or the need for charity. The people of Ghana have worked hard to put democracy on a firmer footing, with peaceful transfers of power even in the wake of closely contested elections. And with improved governance and an emerging civil society, Ghana's economy has shown impressive rates of growth.
>
> This progress may lack the drama of the 20th century's liberation struggles, but make no mistake: it will ultimately be more significant. For just as it is important to

emerge from the control of another nation, it is even more important to build one's own.

To realize that promise, we must first recognize a fundamental truth that you have given life to in Ghana: development depends upon good governance. That is the ingredient which has been missing in far too many places, for far too long. That is the change that can unlock Africa's potential. And that is a responsibility that can only be met by Africans.

Time and again, Ghanaians have chosen Constitutional rule over autocracy, and shown a democratic spirit that allows the energy of your people to break through. We see that in leaders who accept defeat graciously, and victors who resist calls to wield power against the opposition. [...]

But old habits must also be broken. Dependence on commodities – or on a single export – concentrates wealth in the hands of the few, and leaves people too vulnerable to downturns.

In Ghana, for instance, oil brings great opportunities, and you have been responsible in preparing for new revenue. But as so many Ghanaians know, oil cannot simply become the new cocoa.[97]

It is a message which the Ghanaians already knew, and which they have taken to heart. The possibility of commodity wealth is a very real one, and has the potential to permanently alter the future of the country for the better. But it will not be the sole engine of change. Obama was careful in choosing his words in describing what oil brings. It alone does not have the ability to bring about "change" or "improvement", but rather "opportunities" to make those changes and improvements. The resource is simply the key which fits in the lock: it still requires the Ghanaian people to turn it. Caution then is not ill-advised: "Ghana's economy has shown impressive rates of growth," but it has not veered into the same sort of unchecked rise that blighted nations like Nigeria. At the beginning of this chapter the BBC's David Amanor likened Ghana to the baby brother of Nigeria, looking up to it with admiration for what it has done but – as with all younger siblings – silently recognising and learning from its mistakes. Ghana has seen how Nigeria's falling over itself to capitalise on its oil and gas revenue left difficult holes in infrastructure and unanswered questions of its leaders, and is making doubly sure that it does not commit the same mistakes its elder brother did.

There was though palpable excitement across the nation before the official first oil release from the Jubilee field (unofficially oil had been flowing from the field for several weeks, but a date of 15 December was set to allow President John Atta Mills to co-ordinate a great celebration for the arrival of the new resource). The entire ceremony would be broadcast live on Ghanaian television, and a weekend 'Thanksgiving Service' held to thank God for the arrival of first oil in the country. The Ghanaian Air Force marched and luminaries and dignitaries from Ghana and the Jubilee partners (including senior executives at Tullow) were flown by helicopter to the Kwame Nkrumah floating production, storage and offloading (FPSO) platform which was positioned over the Jubilee field to extract its payload. President Mills even managed to bring together the two former Presidents, Jerry Rawlings and John Kuffuor – between whom no love is lost – to celebrate the event. Streaming video was available on Tullow Ghana's website, detailing every aspect of the arrangement for those who were not located in the country. Dai Jones, President and General Manager of Tullow Ghana, quelled the excitement somewhat when he said that "some people think we're going to be the next Saudi Arabia the day after First Oil arrives! But it's very important we try to manage the expectations against reality. Often it's said in the media about Ghana's oil industry and where it's going but reality is we are not an oil industry, we are one oil field which is the first step to creating an oil industry."[98] His was one of the very few realistic voices, however, as Ghanaian jingoism over such a monumental step forward was rightly allowed to dominate the day.

Kuffuor, as ever keen to score political points, was claiming credit for the Jubilee find. "The finds were during my administration. It was my administration that gave the bloc to the two companies that found the Jubilee Fields and joined it together to name it Jubilee. It was under me. So I feel like the parent to the whole situation," he said to national radio station Joy FM on the day of the ceremony. Huge tarpaulins festooned with Ghanaian flag bunting covered some of the most important spectators from the relentless west African heat; offshore the Kwame Nkrumah FPSO was swarming with dignitaries in bright blue overalls with tiny Ghanaian flags sewn on the breast who looked like ants in the labyrinthine scaffolding and vast machinery on the vessel. There was no doubt who was the Anglo-Irish patron of the oil find: the Tullow Oil logo took up most the broad back of the suit in bright white highlights. President Mills inspected a line of Ghanaian guards in full military regalia on the tarmac of Takoradi airbase as a phalanx of press rushed around behind to try and get the best picture for the Ghanaian dailies the following morning. This was a jubilant moment for Jubilee, and a momentous occasion for Ghana. The whole event was carefully orchestrated to look like a Hollywood film – Top Gun for Ghana – with soft-focus close-ups of the lurid yellow helicopter taking off for the Kwame Nkrumah FPSO. Despite government's previously demure attempts to downplay the oil find, every trick was used to present this as a big deal for the nation. And with good reason: handled correctly, Jubilee alone can bring $1 billion to Ghana from production alone each year.[99] With Ghana selling its first ever oil exports a little more than two weeks later, as some of the first Jubilee oil was loaded onto crude oil vessels on New Year's Day 2011 for export to foreign markets through ExxonMobil,[100] this prediction of $1 billion started to look more and more realistic by the day.

Back at the first oil ceremony two weeks previous, Tullow's Keith Mutimer had to give President Mills a final reminder of which direction to turn the valve – "anti-clockwise, Mr President" – as he let first official oil flow just after 10am with a beaming smile. Behind him, the workers celebrated, clenching fists and punching the air. With that, Ghana had entered the league of petrostates, and most probably secured their future as something more than a cocoa state. The worry was that they would replace one commodity with another. Analysts believed that the Ghanaian government had been suitably wary and could manage – and tamp down – expectations. "The oil revenues expected [in Ghana] only represent 6% of their economy. Compare that to Nigeria where oil revenue represents 92% of the economy, or Angola, where it's almost 100%," pointed out Stephen Hayes of the Corporate Council on Africa to the BBC's Focus on Africa, and you begin to realise that those two feared words – resource curse – might not be a self-fulfilling prophecy in Ghana.

"After a long wait, the day has come," said President Mills to the people in prepared remarks back onshore at Takoradi. "But [the oil] means we are assuming a very serious responsibility – and especially for those who are in leadership positions, we must ensure it becomes a blessing, not a curse."[101] 17-year old Brian Salmon, who owns a small patch of land near Takoradi where most of the ballyhoo of the first oil celebrations took place, echoed President Mills' words when interviewed by Reuters. "It will be a blessing because we are all jobless and poor."

The local chamber of commerce organised a three-day course for 45 job seekers in Takoradi the weekend after President Mills turned the tap on the FPSO to learn about the skills required to work in the burgeoning oil industry popping up in the town with the arrival of oil at Jubilee.

While some concerns – such as the possibility of the area around the oil field being overlooked when it comes to benefitting from the proceeds of the resource – were addressed by Mills ("the Western Region where the oil and gas is located will be given pride of place as far as development is concerned," he told those gathered in Takoradi and the television cameras beaming pictures into homes across Ghana. "We want to create jobs to develop our infrastructure; have a robust economy"), other, much larger problems were still to be addressed. The two Petroleum Bills needed to regulate the industry still had not been passed by parliament when the President turned the valve to let first oil flow from Jubilee; one, the Petroleum Commission Bill (which would establish an independent petroleum commission to oversee rights and revenues from oil and gas) was only laid before parliament the day after the Jubilee first oil celebrations. In this instance, Ghana was taking after its elder brother Nigeria more than it would like.

Bright Simons of the IMANI Centre for Policy and Education – an influential thinktank based in Ghana – struck a sombre note on the day of the oil jubilation. "The whole programme seems to have been rushed," she warned. "The rush doesn't benefit anybody. We ought to have been better prepared."[102] The theme of the thanksgiving service held in Accra the weekend after the oil find came from the Proverbs, chapter 24, verses 3 to 6:

> Through wisdom a house is built, and by understanding it is established. By knowledge the rooms are filled with rare and beautiful treasures. A wise man has power – and a man of knowledge increases strength; for by wise counsel you will wage your own war, and in a multitude of counsellors there is safety.

AFRICA

#7 IN WORLD FOR GAS

10% OF ALL WORLD OIL

AT CURRENT RATES, THE CONTINENT HAS

72.4 YEARS

OF GAS REMAINING - 10 MORE THAN ELSEWHERE

SHELL PLAN TO SPEND

$25-27 BILLION BY 2020

$1,600,000,000,000 VALUE OF ECONOMY

RESERVES HAVE GROWN BY

2X THE WORLD AVERAGE

"AFRICAN LIONS" - GORDON BROWN

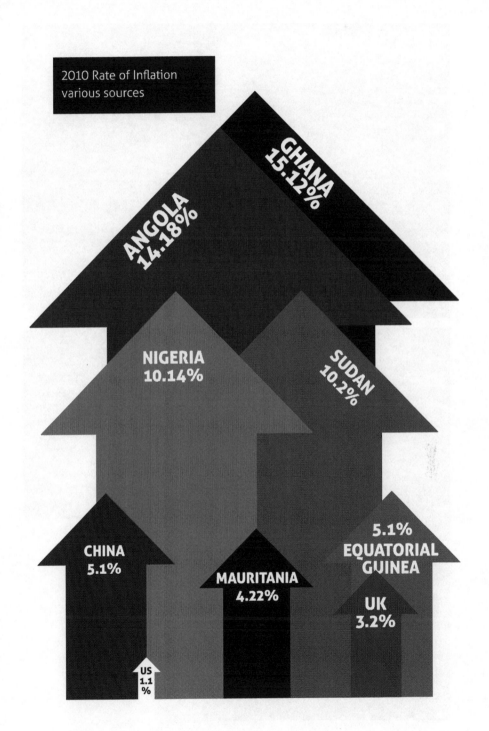

2010 Rate of Inflation
various sources

GHANA
15.12%

ANGOLA
14.18%

NIGERIA
10.14%

SUDAN
10.2%

CHINA
5.1%

MAURITANIA
4.22%

5.1%
EQUATORIAL
GUINEA

UK
3.2%

US
1.1
%

UNITED KINGDOM
79.9 YEARS

ANGOLA
38.2 YEARS

SUDAN
51.4 YEARS

Average life expectancy
(Royal African Society
and national figures)

NIGERIA
46.2 YEARS

MAURITANIA
56.7 YEARS

EQUATORIAL GUINEA
61.6 YEARS

GHANA
58.9 YEARS

UNITED STATES
78.4 YEARS

CHINA
73.1 YEARS

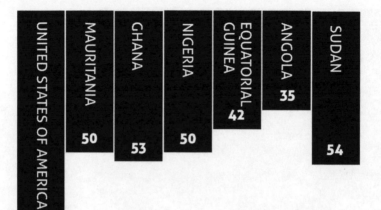

UNITED STATES OF AMERICA

234

MAURITANIA 50

GHANA 53

NIGERIA 50

EQUATORIAL GUINEA 42

ANGOLA 35

SUDAN 54

Years since independence
(as of January 2011)

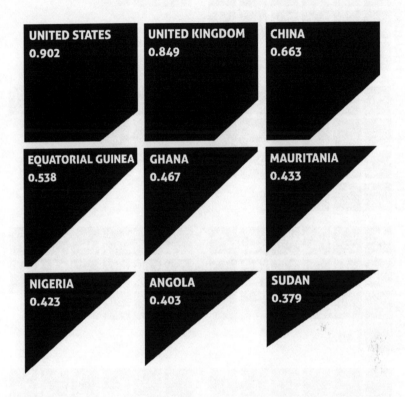

UNITED STATES
0.902

UNITED KINGDOM
0.849

CHINA
0.663

EQUATORIAL GUINEA
0.538

GHANA
0.467

MAURITANIA
0.433

NIGERIA
0.423

ANGOLA
0.403

SUDAN
0.379

UN Human Development Index 2010
0-1 scale

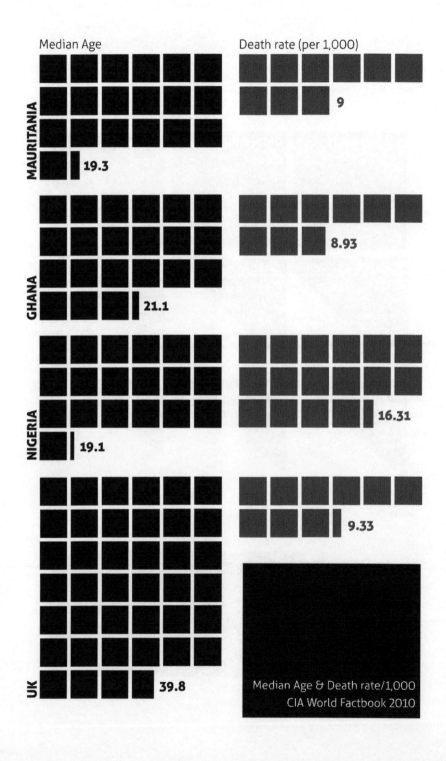

Median Age

Death rate (per 1,000)

MAURITANIA 19.3 9

GHANA 21.1 8.93

NIGERIA 19.1 16.31

UK 39.8 9.33

Median Age & Death rate/1,000
CIA World Factbook 2010

AFRICAN LIONS

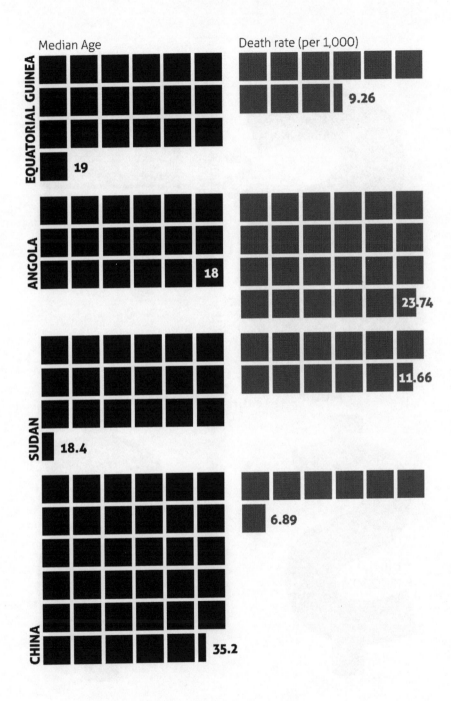

Median Age

Death rate (per 1,000)

EQUATORIAL GUINEA 19 · 9.26

ANGOLA 18 · 23.74

SUDAN 18.4 · 11.66

CHINA 35.2 · 6.89

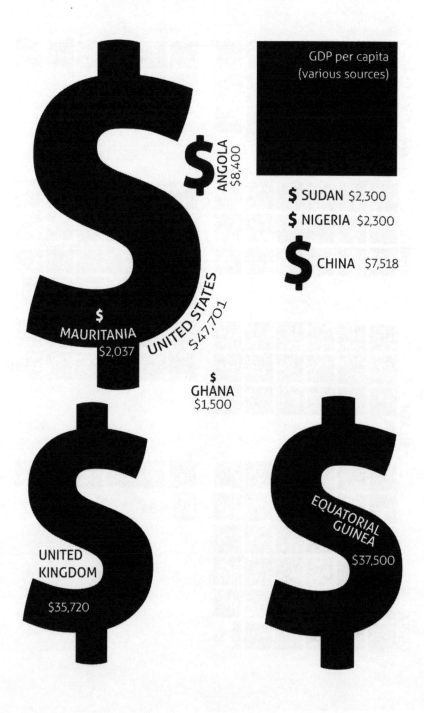

GDP per capita
(various sources)

$ SUDAN $2,300

$ NIGERIA $2,300

$ CHINA $7,518

$ ANGOLA $8,400

$ MAURITANIA $2,037

UNITED STATES $47,701

$ GHANA $1,500

UNITED KINGDOM $35,720

EQUATORIAL GUINEA $37,500

EQUATORIAL
GUINEA
UNITED
STATES

GHANA

MAURITANIA

NIGERIA

Transparency International
Corruption Perceptions Index 2010

ANGOLA
SUDAN
UNITED
KINGDOM
CHINA

Sudan: 1.6
Angola: 1.9
Equatorial Guinea: 1.9
Mauritania: 2.3
Nigeria: 2.4

China: 3.5
Ghana: 4.1
United States: 7.1
United Kingdom: 7.6

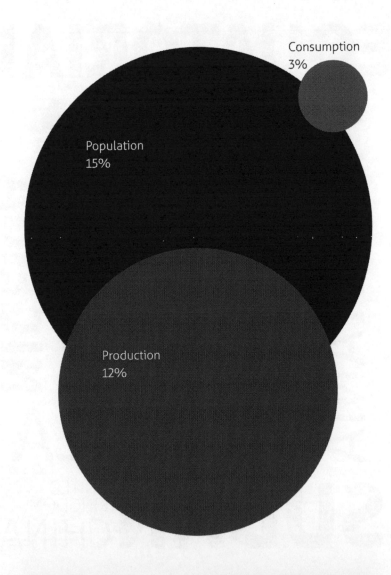

Consumption
3%

Population
15%

Production
12%

African Development Bank 2010
Africa's percentage of the worlds population,
production and consumption

NIGERIA

400%

VALUE LOST ON OIL & GAS DUE TO GOVT CORRUPTION

POPULATION 152,220,000

EUROPE'S LNG SUPPLY

25% NIGERIA

75% REST OF WORLD

$100
MILLION
OF RANSOMS
PAID TO MILITANTS
2006-2008

GOODLUCK
JONATHAN, PRESIDENT

1BILLION
BARRELS/DAY
INTERRUPTED BY MEND ON THE NIGER DELTA

CORRUPTION RIFE

100 MILLION BARRELS OF OIL

MAURITANIA

60% OF THE COUNTRY COVERED BY SAHARA DESERT

SIMILAR IN SIZE TO EGYPT

AL'QAEDA OPERATE IN THE COUNTRY

28 NOVEMBER 1960 INDEPENDENCE DAY

TAOUDENI BASIN

NOUAKCHOTT

GHANA

15 DECEMBER 2010

FIRST OFFICIAL OIL AT JUBILEE

ACCRA

15 MILLION BARRELS OF OIL

JUBILEE

$24,000 AVERAGE WAGE OF GHANA'S MPS

SLOW AND STEADY

60,000 BARRELS PER DAY

$700 AVERAGE GHANAIAN WAGE

EQUATORIAL GUINEA

30%
US' SHARE OF ALL
EQUATOGUINEAN EXPORTS

$1.883
BILLION CURRENT ACCOUNT DEBT

$2B
POTENTIAL
YEARLY PROFIT

10 BATHROOMS, FIVE FIREPLACES, AN INDOOR POOL IN THE MARYLAND PALACE BOUGHT BY PRESIDENT TEODOR OBIANG

90%
OF ALL OIL
PRODUCED GOES TO EXPORT

219 BCM OF OIL
PRODUCED PER YEAR

SOYO

#2 IN AFRICA

ANGOLA

#15
LARGEST OIL
RESERVES IN
THE WORLD

OIL

45% TAX
ON OIL

PAYS MORE
THAN **85%**
OF GDP

PRODUCTION OF 305BCM IN 2014

CHRIS STOKEL-WALKER

When is a bribe not a bribe?

"I have often noticed that a bribe has that effect – it changes a relation. The man who offers a bribe gives away a little of his own importance; the bribe once accepted, he becomes the inferior, like a man who has paid for a woman."

– Graham Greene

In sub-Saharan Africa 41% of people reported to Transparency International's 2010 Global Corruption Barometer that they had paid a bribe to registry and permit services, 20% to the judiciary and 15% to a category defined by the group as 'utilities'. In the European Union respondents gave figures of 3%, 3% and 2% to the same categories. That there is a difference between the west and Africa is to be expected, but is there really that much of a difference in the way we conduct our everyday lives? Or is it just our perception of bribery that is different?

What makes a bribe a bribe? And when is a bribe not a bribe? As has been explored above (and will be explored in later chapters) there are vast cultural differences between the west and Africa, and those differences extend to perceptions of – and definitions of – bribes. 56% of African respondents said they had paid a bribe of some sort in 2010; 5% of EU respondents.

It is likely that the actual difference between the actions of those questioned in Africa and those questioned in the EU is not quite as stark. Rather, our cultural perceptions of what constitutes a bribe inflate the statistical gap.

The sticking point comes in finding the line where a donation (of money, of services or of infrastructure) becomes a bribe. Colonial powers sought to keep natives happier in their entrapment by building roads, hospitals and other vital pieces of infrastructure. Most of them did so in Africa. Oil and gas companies today do the same: a community project, the cornerstone of any self-respecting corporate social responsibility outreach programme, is not all that different from a bribe in cash. The aim of doing so is still to buy off the locals' ire.

Our cultural perception of bribery in the west is that anything directly involving money is bad. Building football pitches or sending locals to universities via bursaries or scholarships are two examples of technical bribery that international companies have used readily in both Africa and the west. Both seek to foster goodwill and show that the 'faceless evil corporation' that many people associate automatically with big business is not all that bad after all. Somehow western perception is that we are comfortable with these kinds of bribes: they are edifying, wholesome and for the cultural good. They are widely reported and widely accepted, held up to be positive parts of a company's actions.

Westerners have an embarrassment about the notion of cash bribes: instead we choose to couch our desire to get things done (whatever the cost) in different terms, believing that we are carrying out some sort of charitable mission – when in reality we are simply currying favour by offering projects for access.

Many Africans do not have the time, the money or the existing basic infrastructure around them to have the luxury of acute embarrassment. Bribery is probably more widespread in Africa than it is in Europe and America, yes, but not by as much as we would like to think it is. Instead they simply go about bribery in a different, more upfront and – to western sensibilities, more tasteless – fashion.

A bribe is anything given from one party to another with the aim (expressed or implicit) to influence, induce or persuade someone of something. It just so happens that in the west we are more comfortable inducing people with great public works rather than an electronic transfer to an offshore bank account.

In Africa cash-in-hand bribes are the norm: then-Nigerian Attorney General Michael Aondoakaa actively sought $20 million in payment ($2 million that day and $18 million the next) to sign a single document, leaked US diplomatic cables allege. A two-year ban on practicing under the title of Senior Advocate of Nigeria was later meted down to Aondoakaa after he was removed from the post of Attorney General.[103] He was officially declared "a persona non grata for offences relating to corruption" in June 2010, but his case is not unique. Across governments and judiciaries in many African countries bribes are openly solicited: in many places, they are often the only recourse for companies or individuals wanting things to be done quickly. A Chatham House report on bribery in Nigeria found that "one British executive working in the oil industry says his company routinely pays immigration officials a bribe worth between 20 and 30 per cent of the cost of expatriate resident permits"[104] in order to circumvent the difficulties that such an oil company might find in trying to bring foreign workers into Nigeria given government's professed strict quotas on jobs for local people.

In Europe too bribes are used to win over locals protesting the building of a pipeline near their homes, or to encourage governments to act faster on reading planning documents and opening public consultations. The promise of investment in a local or national economy by buying books for children, or building a new community hall, has much the same effect as money does. It tries (and often does) influence people in the bribers' favour.

Shell used the more obvious cash-in-hand method when bribing local subcontractors $2 million to help give it an "improper advantage" when building its Bonga project 75 miles offshore the Niger Delta.[105] US investigators found that from the $2 million initial layout to local workers, Shell gained to the tune of $14 million through access to the near-600 million barrels of oil estimated to lie under the Bonga field. Eni, as Tullow's Regional Vice President for Africa Tim O'Hanlon was reported in US embassy cables to have claimed, have also engaged in bribing ministers in Uganda for preferential access to hydrocarbon reserves and a less problematic bureaucratic process in gaining immigration papers, drilling rights and shipping allowances at all stages of projects. As explained below, the near-entirety of Angola and Equatorial Guinea's oil and gas industry works under blatant bribery, rather than legal contracts.

Should western companies be concerned at this? Or should they accept that open bribes are simply part of the culture in Africa? In essence, our great colonial mission succeeded: we gave Africa the impression that commodity imperialism – taking wantonly from the land without repaying in kind the inhabitants of that land – was the way business was done. The vision of democracy presented by us was only half-formed: we gave them an unfinished version, whereby all the full features of a true democracy (accountability, independence and transparency) are not present, which was presented as the whole. Colonial celebratists will say that colonialism 'did good' – that it proved edifying for a supposedly previously-uncouth people. But colonial powers only demonstrated a version of the western world which had been reconfigured to ensure that the west ruled all. Lacking in the taught version of 'culture' and 'society' (which colonialists thought was the only real culture or society that could be brooked) were any oversights. That manifests itself in corrupt governments, half-formed infrastructure, domineering despots and a more open system of bribery. The only difference between the west and Africa when it comes to bribery is, to many eyes, one of naming. While drillers in the west use implicit bribes through community projects, African officials are more open and less duplicitous about their openness to being swayed by bribes. We seek in the west to place Africa's preponderance of bribes in a postcolonial prism to such an extent that we ignore that it is little different to the way our business operates.

There is one key difference, though. Corporate social responsibility schemes are more difficult to fudge. A school cannot be misused as much as a million-dollar bank transfer, and is more likely to go towards the intended target: the people. It is still a bribe, just as it would be if an international oil company were to build a community centre in Maidstone rather than Mpogo, Uganda. But it is a bribe which has worth to the people, and is less likely to foster corruption. "African companies are still waking up to the potential of CSR as a positive force in the shaping of the continent's economic future. The opportunity is there to give something back to the continent. But CSR initiatives worthy of the name need to be more than just marketing tools to increase the visibility of multinationals' brands in Africa," writes Marieme Jamme.[106] They also need to not be poorly-disguised rehashes of the half-hearted projects that colonial powers began and often abandoned throughout the continent.

In countries like Angola that are known (as will be found out below) to be particularly poor in terms of governance, such CSR initiatives are often directly acknowledged to be responsible for companies' access to oil and gas reserves. Total SA funded three projects by the Angolan Environmental Ministry at a cost of $5.5 million on behalf of them and the other companies operating in Block 17 in Angola, an oil-rich area which includes the Dalia field (able to produce between 200,000 and 250,000 barrels per day). Angola's Environmental Minister Fatima Jardim "considered the projects as fundamental"[107] to the improvement of the country – and likely thought the funding fundamental to Total's continued good practice in Angola too.

Western countries are still reticent, a hangover of their colonial thinking past; a squeamishness which China and other eastern economies hold less important in considering their trade links with the continent. Chinese officials have fewer problems with human rights laxity and will and have turned a blind and unblinking eye to corruption. He Wenping, Director of African Studies at Beijing's Institute of West Asian and African Studies notes that in some respects African governments prefer China because the "Chinese are less critical of their internal political affairs, and there's less bureaucracy so projects and deals are executed a lot faster."[108] They do not have the decades of prejudice and memories of a subservient, incapable Africa that the western former colonists almost invariably do.

In discussions with the west African officials can be scathing about China, but the reality is that despite the more pressing concern that China will dominate them more than any western economy ever would they much prefer the eastern governments to the west and are simply trying to keep both paths open, an expediency which stands the future of African oil and gas in good stead. Members of the Nigerian National Petroleum Corporation (NNPC) spoke detrimentally of the

Chinese to an American Embassy official in Abuja, as reported in a leaked December 2009 cable. "The Chinese are very aggressive because they need the oil," the NNPC representative explained. "They do not know how to deal with a democratic government. [...] The Chinese caused the problem," he went on, "and they ruffled a lot of feathers."[109] Of course, the reality is that impropriety has been rife in the African – and particularly Nigerian – gas and oil industries for decades, and is not simply the product of China's entrance in the market. Earlier we saw how Shell were involved in endemic corruption and bribery of governments in Nigeria alone, predating the Chinese interest in Nigeria's resources by almost a decade or more.

What is different – and what can be taken from the NNPC's representatives remarks – is the approach that each potential partner takes, and the way in which African officials are forced to act towards each side. While the NNPC can openly talk of bribery and corruption to Chinese counterparts because of the similar indifferent outlook that each side holds, they must take the outraged stance of the west towards overt bribery when meeting with them.

The China-Africa trade link is an important one for both sides, a point that the Chinese were keen to make clear in a white paper the Chinese Cabinet released on China-Africa Economic and Trade Cooperation.[110] According to figures proclaimed in the white paper, total two-way trade between China and Africa was valued at a staggering $114.8 billion between January and November 2010 – 43.5% higher than the same period of time the year previous. The 29 pages of the paper established just how vitally China viewed Africa as a trading partner and sought to crow their qualities, wooing the relatively young but potentially massive continent in a way that the west are too reticent to do. China's 'don't ask, don't tell' attitude and its ability to undercut prices on almost any infrastructure it offers to build for African nations has resulted in more than half of all the open public works contracts across the whole continent being won by Chinese companies. As to whether all of these contracts were won fairly and without bribery, it seems unlikely, but one thing is certain: for African governments, China is now the trade partner of choice.

Everywhere throughout the Chinese white paper is a sense of commonality which cannot or would seem forced from the mouths of a western government, given our chequered past with the continent: "China-Africa economic and trade cooperation is a major component of South-South cooperation, infuses new life into the latter, and elevates the political and economic status of developing countries in the world, playing a significant role in promoting the establishment of a fair and rational new international political and economic order," the Cabinet write. Implicit within this is a sense of stoking the fear of western colonialism and a nod towards common (sometimes less than perfect) practice when it comes to negotiations. China is everywhere: "investment in Africa is distributed in 49 African countries," the paper explains. In at least three of those 49 countries, no-questions-asked Chinese investment is propping up the vestiges of dictatorial military rule, while keeping the general populace – who should by rights be benefitting from the quantifiably enormous natural resources their land contains – in thrall to the leaders who have little interest beyond their own gains, and seek to perpetuate the supposed inferiority of the African continent.

Mauritania, Angola and Equatorial Guinea

"Cabinet Ministers and public servants in Equatorial Guinea are by law allowed to own companies that, in consortium with a foreign company, can bid for government contracts. But, in any event, it means that a cabinet minister ends up with a sizeable part of the contract price in his bank account. It is in the context, therefore, of the law of Equatorial Guinea that my owning a company should be viewed by this court."

– Teodorin Obiang, Equatoguinean Forestry Minister, sworn affidavit

Mauritania's first oil production is relatively recent in comparison to other African countries: in February 2006 its Chinguetti oil field, 56 miles offshore south west of the capital city Nouakchott began producing oil. Only 12km^2 in size, Chinguetti was discovered in 2001 and has over 20 exploration, appraisal and development wells. Within two weeks of pumping first oil from the ground, the field had reached production of 75,000 barrels of oil a day; a week later Chinguetti had already produced a million barrels of oil, which were promptly sent in its first shipment to China.

Bolstered by the early success of Chinguetti, Minister of Oil and Energy Zeidane Ould Hmeida (the first head of the Mauritanian Oil and Energy Ministry since its founding in March 2005) and his successor Wane Ibrahima Lamine have overseen rapid exploration and development of other fields including the Tiof, Banda and Pelican fields; the Tiof field, 16 miles north of Chinguetti, has produced similarly successful exploratory results. The CIA World Factbook estimated in 2010 that the country has 100 million barrels of proven oil reserves and 28.32 billion cubic metres (bcm) of gas.

Two companies in recent years have also looked into the possibility of housing an LNG facility in Mauritania. Shell in 2009 and GDF-Suez in 2006 sought agreement with the Mauritanian government to build an LNG facility near Nouakchott, with the eventual aim of using the country as a base from which to export LNG cargoes to Europe and the US. However the amount of gas needed to economically run an LNG facility meant that the offshore gas fields explored then and still currently being explored are not – to the minds of companies – sufficient to demand such a plant. The country though does have significant inland assets which could be exploited inland near the Sahara desert (which stretches across almost 60% of the nation), with the government pinning great hopes on the great white sands of the Taoudeni Basin.

To an outsider the concept of gas and oil drilling in the Sahara may seem like a laughable concept: remote and unforgiving, the terrain itself is enough reason to dissuade most from exploring its riches. However underneath the Sahara is a largely untapped wealth of resources, and there is precedence in nearby Algeria to prove that a desert climate does not preclude successful hydrocarbon production. Indeed Total SA announced in late September 2010[111] that they would be the first company to investigate the possibility of oil and gas in the Taoudeni Basin, committing to an agreement to explore the area with Energy Minister Wane Ibrahima Lamine. Additionally, while Algeria may prove a model of how successful desert drilling can be, it – like Nigeria – has been plagued by infighting and widespread terrorism, causing disruptions to its drilling and production plans and pushing international oil companies away from its borders and into the arms of Mauritania. Because of its comparative youth in the oil and gas area, Mauritania has yet to receive the backlash from the general populace to any potential resource colonialism, nor has it yet attracted the same level of attention of opportunistic terrorist groups looking to capitalise on the spoils of gas and oil revenue which would undoubtedly flow into the country upon an increase in production.

Mauritania is well positioned, then, to offer gas and oil via sea and pipeline to a variety of markets, and has seen international interest from a huge number of companies, especially since it joined the Extractive Industries Transparency Initiative (EITI) in September 2007. Petronas, Wintershall, RWE, Repsol, Total, GDF-Suez, Eni and SEPCA have all expressed an interest in the country's oil and gas sector and backed it up with financial investment in projects.

While Mauritania may well seem like the attractive and peaceful alternative to the war-torn Algeria, it too has its own share of problems. It currently is under military rule after the first democratically elected President in the country's independent history and his government were deposed in a coup led by General Mohamed Ould Abdel Aziz on 6 August 2008, a year and a half after they came to power. Prior to (and since) those 17 months of true democracy, Mauritania had alternated between single party politics and de facto military dictatorship since gaining its independence from France in November 1960. As a result of the 2008 coup the World Bank removed a promised $413 million loan that was to be paid to the country in instalments from 2008 to 2011. The US also immediately withdrew an aid programme worth $25 million to the country and the EU cancelled more than $150 million in planned lending to Mauritania. There was – and still is, despite Aziz resigning from his military post and running (and winning) a subsequent (greatly flawed) 2009 election – a worldwide wariness in giving Mauritania too much unqualified aid given its military governmental past. Only Iran, Morocco and Libya were left supporting the post-coup Mauritania under Aziz, largely because the new President disavowed the country's relationship with Israel. The ousted President, Sidi Ould Cheikh Abdallahi was placed under house arrest and forced to resign his post officially to allow the July 2009 election to take place, which returned Aziz to government with a 52% majority.

Mauritania relied heavily on international aid, meaning that the impetus to diversify its revenues was great for Aziz's ruling party almost as soon as he gained power. Taking on the work done by the previous government in hydrocarbon promotion, Aziz has accelerated negotiations with international drillers and producers in an attempt to make up the shortfall in the nation's finances. Buoyed by the backing of the electorate to produce a mandate (despite the fact that many observers believe that casual, if not necessarily centralised controlled pressure was placed on voters to return Aziz to power) and a technical legitimacy, the new President has been able to negotiate access to his oil and gas fields with outside countries and interested parties from a position of power which many other African leaders are lacking.

President Aziz is still struggling with terrorism problems of his own, though admittedly not based around natural resources like the problems the Nigerian government face on a daily basis. Al-Qaeda militants are present and planning their future in the seclusion of the Sahara desert and have instigated a spate of killings and kidnappings of non-governmental organisation workers and volunteers connected to international aid companies. In response to this Aziz turned in the middle of 2010 to a peculiarly colonial solution to the problem: strict delineation of the Mauritanian territorial borders and a closing-off of access to the country for foreigners. By Presidential decree 45 border stations were set up to control the migration of people in and out of Mauritania, and immigration laws were strengthened to allow rapid deportation of illegal immigrants. "We are prepared to sacrifice everything for the sake of security," announced Defence Minister Hamadi Ould Baba Ould Hamadi, following it with an extraordinary admission. "It is our number one priority – ahead of development and democracy."[112]

Prioritising security over development and democracy may sound like a shocking tactic, but it perversely may be the best way to prepare the ground for an amenable environment that international oil and gas companies can work in (and from that create a better basis on which to build a democracy). On a continent in which the race to reach democratic freedom first almost matches the speed at which colonialists in the 19th century and now seek to divide up Africa between them, Mauritania's admittance that rapidity might not be the best course of action is startlingly brave. While damaging in the short term for human rights and growth, the hope is that ensuring a firm foundation of security (*The Economist*'s 2010 business risk index placed Mauritania tied-32nd of 180 risky countries[113]) is present before tackling the difficult transition from dictatorship to democracy will help make the passage easier in the long run. It also may prove a refreshing counterbalance to Nigeria's chaotic and broken democracy for potential investors to know that Aziz has the will and the might to crack down on insurgency in a way that leaders such as Goodluck Jonathan have been unwilling. Mauritania's government, moreso than other leaders, seem to acknowledge that in Africa democracy is not yet an either-or concept but rather must be considered in shades of grey for the time being.

*   *   *

Roughly 1500 years ago what is now known as Mauritania was Berber land, home to indigenous people to the area who had their own tribal cultures and languages. They survived in the region for nearly a thousand years until the Arabian Beni Hassan tribe invaded and conquered the Berbers, bringing with them the Arabic customs and language that the Islamic Republic of Mauritania (to give the country its full name) still live by today. Alongside new customs, a new and acute awareness of social standing, particularly in relation to race, was brought into Mauritanian culture.

This complicated the already impenetrable social mores of tribal culture that exist in Africa to today; following Arabian invasion a multi-faceted structure of power was established that saw Arab take precedence over African, and the language spoken and colour of skin became a determining power in the level of society any given person could attain to. The ruling fair-skinned Arabs were masters, and their slaves were predominately black natives. There were some steps towards integration, however: "on their arrival into the region, the Muslim conquerors intermarried with local people, giving rise to the heterogeneous mix of people found in Mauritania today," Max de Vietri writes in his study of Mauritania's past.[114] These Berber-Arab people maintained a strong sense of tribalism – "traits [that] continue to affect the political and institutional structure of Mauritania to this day."

As with the example of Ghana, large parts of the population took to colonialism when it arrived in the 18th century with a grim acceptance and eagerness to make the most of an unfortunate situation. Black Mauritanians learnt from their French colonisers the value of administration and the French language; like most colonies, this taste of western development led to a yearning to escape from colonisation and to move towards self-governance. The Arab section of the populace still retained their tribal roots and shunned the democratic movement that was growing strong amongst urbane French-speaking black Mauritanians. Independence was gained from France on 28 November 1960, and on 20 August 1961 Mokhtar Ould Daddah was named Mauritania's first President. Daddah almost immediately took the country into the United Nations and established an iron ore and fishing industry, created a capital city and ruling infrastructure, all while trying to fend off the claims of Morocco to the country (Morocco eventually reneged and recognised Mauritania as an independent state in 1969, almost a decade after the rest of the world). President Daddah's rush to exploit Mauritania's sea for fishing – and the resultant overfishing by Japanese, Russian and Spanish fleets – has acted as a cautionary tale for current President Aziz's stance on access to his country's natural resources by international drilling companies.

Daddah's rallying cry to the new nation was "let's build the Mauritanian homeland together!" Little did he know how much Mauritania's pre-colonial history had formed deeply entrenched societal beliefs, and how France's preferential colonial rule to the black Berbers, rather than the Arabs, had calcified relations. The President was an Arab himself, and sought five years into his rule to make bilingual teaching compulsory in the Mauritanian education system. He pushed through a Presidential decree which saw the capital Nouakchott become the scene of interracial violence as the three different ethnic groups (Arabian moors, black Africans and the mixed-race group, each of whom make up roughly equal parts of the population) battled over this first sign of ethnic difficulties. While Daddah's aims were good, in trying to create a fair and equal nation, like the colonial leaders before him in countries across Africa he underestimated the deep divides between disparate groups and overestimated the ease with which a leader can bring them into one common-thinking nation. Still strong in the minds of those black Mauritanians that took to the streets over schools was the five hundred years of slavery they had endured, first under Arab invaders then white colonisers. Under an Arab President, they feared that teaching the Arabian language equally alongside the native French was the first step towards a third colonisation.

The fear is there, then, that hydrocarbon colonisation would be not a second-stage colonisation as it is in most African countries, but potentially a fourth wave of control in the eyes of black native Mauritanians. President Mohamed Ould Abdel Aziz (though as his name suggests, an Arab Mauritanian) is aware of the fear that pervades black Mauritanian thinking over this and seems careful to not allow his nation to endure further subjugation.

Aziz also knows that to take advantage of the potentially massive amount of natural resources that sit under Mauritanian soil he must assure international drilling companies that his country is safe and stable. While not currently fighting a pitched-battle war against militants like President Goodluck Jonathan in Nigeria, Aziz has to carefully balance race and interfaith relations to ensure that the volatility which the country has experience in the past does not flare up once again. From the mid-1980s to the mid-1990s Mauritania experienced firsthand this kind of conflict, and it scuppered the first migration of oil and gas producers into the country, who left the resources in the ground and abandoned the country to its in-fighting.

Mauritanian Prime Minister Lieutenant-Colonel Maaouya Ould Sid'Ahmed Taya had been elected to his post in March 1981 by then-President Mohamed Khouna Ould

Haidallah in an attempt to shore up his military support following an unsuccessful coup by black African dissidents within the military. Prime Minister Taya acted as a crutch for the increasingly isolated President Haidallah, whose Arab support was waning. When Haidallah left the country for a meeting of French-speaking African nations in Burundi on 12 December 1984, Taya took advantage of his widespread black African public support (and Haidallah's unpopularity) to launch a bloodless coup and take the mantle of President of Mauritania. As can be expected from a country with such a long and chequered history of interracial relations, Taya's taking of the Presidency from an Arabian – and his leniency and pacifism towards the black African population, who many Arabs believed should be deported – angered the Arab sectors of the populace. Tensions escalated, and protest groups were established, which rapidly transformed into racial militias.

One such group was the Front de Liberation des Africains en Mauritanie (FLAM) who represented the black population. In protest at the Arab dominance of government – and in spite of President Taya's beneficence towards them in the face of large anger from his own Arab community – they and other black pressure groups launched an attempted coup. Taya lost patience. Hundreds of his former supporters (all black Africans) were rounded up and executed. By 1989 mobs controlled the streets in Mauritania and Senegal, engaging in tit-for-tat conflict. Attempts to quieten the discord resulted in some quarter of a million black Africans of the Bidan tribe being deported from Senegal and Mauritania. In 1990 Taya turned his back on Mauritanian ideals that the country was a split-race nation that could co-exist peacefully and called it a purely Arab country, altering the constitution to say so. This volte-face, combined with interracial violence and government support for the Iraqi regime under Saddam Hussein on religious grounds during the First Gulf War meant that foreign investors shied away from the potential lucre that could come from Mauritania's reserves underfoot. They would only begin to consider returning to Mauritania half a decade later, when Taya – still in power thanks to a 1992 democratic election which saw tribal leaders influence up to 70% of the vote by some estimates – curbed his more extreme stances on international relations.

Taya was to stay in power, surviving successive coups and elections (where he routinely won nearly 70% of the popular vote), until the Mauritanian military deposed him in November 2005, while he attended the funeral of Saudi King Fahd bin Abdul Aziz. They "unanimously decided," they declared, "to put a definitive end to the oppressive activities of the defunct authority" that they "suffered" under. An election, a coup and another election later, current President Aziz is trying to present a stable front to what has been an unstable – but non-violent for nearly 20 years now – country.

It was the excessive violence and unpredictability of previous regimes which unsettled foreign investment in the oil and gas sector. President Aziz's determination to nip violence in the bud, and expel Al'Qaeda from the Saharan sections of the country (at the expense of everything else, including political freedom and national development) has opened the door for countries who once viewed Mauritania with fear and loathing to return to its land. Currently the country is a marginal player at best in the African hydrocarbon world – it only crept into the status of being a net oil exporter in 2006 having spent the best part of a decade importing nearly 25,000 more barrels of oil than it exported, despite its vast reserves. Like many African countries, the problem is one of control over the chaos which reigns within its borders, and an attempt to balance the need to ensure that such instability is dealt with whilst also trying to develop sound infrastructure on which to promote its resources. Mauritania is similar to size in Egypt, but is a world away from having its infrastructure and technology (though it must be noted that as is the case in much of Africa, democracy is still a word which has many different interpretations. Egypt's most recent parliamentary elections in November 2010 were beset with allegations of voter fraud and widespread protests ensued as President Hosni Mubarak clung onto power as January 2011 gave way to February. At the print deadline of *African Lions*, Egypt's infighting, focused around the ironically-named Tahrir (Freedom) Square had turned horrifically violent, killing at least 13 (though unofficial estimates said upwards of 30 or more had actually been killed) and 1,200 injured (though Dr Ibrahim Fata, a doctor on the scene, claimed more than 2,000 wounded) as pro- and anti-Mubarak supporters clashed for the first day after a week of comparatively peaceful protest).

Mauritania did once seem to be on the verge of being a hydrocarbon nation. Twenty years of exploration by foreign investors had reaped some rewards, but the violence of the mid- and late-1980s discouraged companies from taking further steps on successful exploration drilling. They returned in the late 1990s for another attempt at drilling, but political expediency on behalf of the government in a vain attempt to divert attention from their own failings once again discouraged companies including Woodside Petroleum, who drilled the Chinguetti well but divested themselves of Mauritanian interests after they and then-Energy Minister Zeidane Ould Hmeida were accused of "lies, corruption and collusion". This was during the state of flux which held the country between its coups and elections at the start of this century. Only now that some semblance of order has been restored by President Aziz do international companies seem to once more be looking at the possibility of using Mauritania to diversify their assets in Africa.

A note of caution must be struck, however. As Max de Vietri warns, "the presence of civilian figures in today's military government is easily overestimated, and their positions are likely to be maintained purely for reasons of balancing assignments to administrative positions between the tribes in order to maintain the status quo. Today, no matter how many technocrats or civilians are appointed to posts in the government, the military is still the power running the country.

Outsiders wishing to [do] business in Mauritania must be aware of this fact when developing relationships with government representatives and in finding champions who can promote projects at the highest echelons of power."

De Vietri calls the part-tribal, part-military, part-democratic makeup of Mauritania an 'ethnic tribal democracy', a technical democracy "built around ethnic loyalties" which mean that a two-tier system prevails whereby the Arab population controls most levels of government and business, keeping the black African population in informal, unspoken thrall. It is, de Vietri explains, "not expressly written in the constitution, nor is it incorporated into any written laws, but it is clearly understood by all". Indeed, for all the talk in previous chapters of Nigeria's high levels of corruption and bias, Transparency International's Corruption Perceptions Index of 2010 found Mauritania marginally more corrupt than Nigeria, 2.3 to 2.4 (where the lower the number on a scale to 10, the more corrupt).

Sadly the need to rely on bribes to ensure the quick movement of projects is still needed in Mauritania, where bribery is built-in to the culture. Many Mauritanians consider gifts (such as those that the first colonisers gave to tribal leaders to ensure they would not protest too loudly to the impending appropriation of local workers and resources) as not being unethical per se. Many do, however – as can be seen with the pursuit of Woodside Petroleum over bribes paid – see the payment of cash to ensure access to land to be against better judgement. Mauritania is almost alone in the oil-rich countries of West Africa in being a nation where cash bribes will not be welcomed as openly as one might expect. The practice is a new one that stems directly, de Vietri posits, from the influx of oil and gas companies believing that what works in the rest of Africa must automatically apply to Mauritania.

Tribes are willing to accept development grants, though, much as in the western world great play is put on corporate social responsibility. Tribes in Mauritania, much like most of the rest of Africa, still control much of the country below governmental level. Woodside found difficulty in refusing to enter into the complicated mesh of tribal politics when they needed the goodwill of the people to promulgate the potential importance of oil and gas discoveries to the nation. De Vietri, ever the expert on Mauritania from his access to high-level negotiations in the hydrocarbon sector with the country, points out that "the company would have been more effective if it had sought a business patron from an influential tribe."

There are, though, countries that find bribery much more amenable as recompense for access to their resources – and they seem less worried about the prospect of a new wave of hydrocarbon colonialism. To find them, you need to travel several hundred miles south.

*   *   *

Tied 168th of 178 countries on the 2010 Transparency International Corruption Perceptions Index are Angola and Equatorial Guinea, placed into the same bracket of corruption as Iraq, Afghanistan and Somalia, whose huge number of piracy attacks have made the headlines of western news bulletins in a way that Nigeria's MEND skirmishes and kidnappings as yet have not. Angola is a country similar in size to Mauritania that sits in the south of the continent. Equatorial Guinea takes up slightly more than 10,000 square miles in the small nook eked out between Cameroon and Gabon.

Equatorial Guinea has been under the rule of President Teodoro Obiang Nguema Mbasogo since 1979. He declared the country a democracy (though only in name) in 1991, and held elections in 1996, 2002 and 2009 – which he won with 95.8% of the vote. Very few observers believe that voters had much choice with their ballot. Angola has staggered out of a 27-year long civil war and has a President, Jose Eduardo Dos Santos, who is withholding an election until his country thrashes out a new constitution. Both have disproportionately high levels of natural gas and oil within their borders: Angola holds the fifteenth largest proven oil reserves in the whole world[115] (at 13.5 billion barrels) and has 960 billion cubic metres (bcm) of gas – the second largest reserves in sub-Saharan Africa behind Nigeria; Equatorial Guinea, belying its small geographical footprint, has more than a billion barrels of oil and some 36 billion cubic metres of gas. Startlingly, though Equatorial Guinea currently only holds 0.1% of the world's proven reserves according to the BP 2010 Statistical Review of Energy, analysts believe that with a thorough and modern geological survey of the country's on- and off-shore assets that share of the world's reserves could rocket to nearly 10% of the global total.

Realising this the US have managed to keep a strong presence (taking 30% of Equatorial Guinea's exports) in the country through companies like ExxonMobil, conveniently turning a blind eye to President Obiang's corrupt practices, managing to solicit hundreds of thousands of barrels of oil each day, largely to the benefit of their own coffers. Obiang is publicly said to be unhappy with the arrangements, even though he profits from the arrangements more than most. Recent estimates indicate that the country should be receiving between $2 billion and $3 billion in profits yearly[116] (in a country whose current account balance is $1.883 billion in debit) for allowing foreign drillers access to its oil and gas reserves, but Obiang's shrewdness and double-dealing means that most of the profits from drilling go into shoring up his military might to keep down any potential uprisings and personal vanity projects, while the general population remain in deep poverty.

Equatorial Guinea exports minimal amounts of LNG to Chile, France and Portugal (roughly 11% of all exports) but the lion's share of their gas trade is with Asia. Like Nigeria and Ghana, Equatorial Guinea has been wooed by favourable rates and long-term loans provided by Asian trade partners, particularly Japan and South Korea, to whom together it exports 68% of its total LNG. As would be expected from such a desperately poor nation with an expedient leader, President Obiang has few qualms about the potential for an international takeover of his nation as long as they continue to plunge money into his pockets. A 2004 investigation by the US Senate found that an American company, Riggs Bank, was involved in the regular sloughing off of oil revenues for Equatoguinean officials.[117] Riggs Bank handled accounts containing $700 million for the government, including the personal accounts of President Obiang, for whom the bank located a palatial house in Maryland with ten bathrooms, five fireplaces and an indoor pool, bought for $2.6 million in cash. Sarah Wykes of the non-governmental organisation Global Witness said of the corruption in the country that "since oil came on stream, the human development indicators of the country have actually gone backward. The oil money is not contributing to development at all." Sadly the current situation in Equatorial Guinea is of benefit to both the government and producers, meaning that any serious change in regime or practices surrounding the exploitation of gas and oil in the country is unlikely to happen soon.

Angola is much the same. Reliant on oil and gas production for nearly 85% of its GDP, the country is more than willing to welcome foreign investment in the hydrocarbon sector as long as bribes are paid and funds siphoned off to the higher ranking officials. Regulatory regimes in both countries are, as would be expected, more lax than most on the rest of the continent, never mind the world. Again Angola has made trading pacts with China and the US who are willing to tolerate bad practices for less restricted access to resources which look to keep the country dependent on foreign investment in a re-run of colonial practices. Indeed Angola export more than 90% of the sum of their nation's oil production (between 1.7 and 1.9 million barrels per day[118]), mainly to the twin superpowers of the US and China, who take upwards of 500,000 barrels per day each. This rapid expansion has meant that in 2009 Angola became the largest crude oil producing country in Africa, supplanting Nigeria whose problems with terrorism and insurgency in the Niger Delta caused their production to slump. Additionally natural gas in the country, currently intertwined with oil production, will be stepped up dramatically in line with oil according to the Angolan government, with plans to export the majority of associated gas (produced as a by-product of oil drilling) via LNG by 2012.

The Angola LNG project in Soyo, situated in the north of the country is a joint venture between state-owned Sonangol, Chevron, BP, Total SA and Eni. Initial estimates have placed the processing volume of Angola LNG at a billion cubic feet of gas per day, some to be used domestically while the majority would be exported to the United States and China. While many such projects are plagued by delays in delivery, meaning that the 2012 deadline for the plant to be built and running would ordinarily be speculative, the severity of the Angolan regime under President Dos Santos indicates that such a timeframe is realistic. In the past Dos Santos and his country have come under severe criticism from human rights organisations and the United Nations for its systematic use of imprisonment, killings, torture and rape to ensure the timely completion of gas and oil projects; Dos Santos meanwhile has defended these practices publicly, claiming they are necessary and justified by the need to profit from Angola's natural resources.

Sonangol was established in 1976 and since 1978 has been in sole control of the upstream oil sector in Angola, meaning any international company wishing to gain access to Angola's plentiful oil fields must enter into a joint venture or production sharing agreement with the company. Issues have been readily pointed out for decades as to the problems with having a single state-owned entity responsible for access to reserves while also seeking to profit themselves from the exploitation of those reserves: Sonangol's best commercial interests may well conflict with the best interests of the country. Angola's opaque political system has been aware of this potential conflict of interests but operates on the same standards, seemingly unwilling to make access to oil fair for all. For international companies seeking to enter Angola, then, Sonangol must be won over to achieve anything. The benefits though are palpable – an International Energy Agency study in 2006[119] found that the average level of tax paid on oil profits is between 45-50%, while in Nigeria nearly 80% tax is levied on international companies.

President Dos Santos has created a state under his personal control with attractive terms for international drillers, attempting to make plentiful profit on his country's natural resources. A 2007 report[120] by French charity Comité Catholique contre la Faim et pour le Développement (CCFD) found that Dos Santos "is frequently associated with corruption and the embezzlement of oil in Angola, and his family has a vast pool of wealth, including houses in major European capitals, and bank accounts in Switzerland and other tax havens," demonstrating why he is quite so welcoming to foreign revenue streams. "In 2004 *Le Monde* reported," the charity's paper continues, "President Dos Santos and his relatives diverted a quarter of all state resources – averaging $1.7 billion per year – between 1997 and 2001." So great is the concern about money laundering that the Angolan Embassy's accounts in Washington DC were closed in 2010 over banks' fears of being used in the fraud. Whether the people of Angola resent constant resource colonialism is a moot point: Dos Santos' single party de facto dictatorship is encouraging of large foreign investment, chaining the country's potential future development to international investment for the foreseeable future.

The Angolan Petroleum Law of 2004 does encourage development in Angola, including in its wording requirements that international companies "include Angolan citizens at every level of staff providing they possess the required expertise" and "support the professional education of Angolans", but both clauses are poorly enforced and have been deliberately constructed as to be vague enough to allow little international action in response to its breaking. Additionally, the International Energy Agency report found, "under some contracts the partners in a particular block are obliged to devote a percentage of the block's revenues to fund corporate social responsibility (CSR) activities" – but again the percentage required to be siphoned off to local authorities is not specified, and "most companies note that they plan their CSR activities in consultation with the Angolan authorities." With CSR money handed over to local officials, and the distribution of such monies controlled by the Angolan authority rather than left to the discretion of the international oil companies, most neutral observers cast doubt on whether the majority of the funds are used to help communities at all.

The political system in Angola is so muddled and opaque that Angolan citizens are unsure of the level of complicity of foreign investors in keeping funds away from the people and in the hands of government officials. They therefore react with anger – but powerlessness – towards both President Dos Santos and international companies in equal measure. Sadly, the political climate means this is highly unlikely to change, and oil and gas companies must enter Angola in the knowledge that they will be blamed for propping up a dictatorship and its supporters with financial aid and a loan of legitimacy, while also perpetuating the commodity colonialism which the ordinary people of Africa so vociferously abhor.

That the Angola LNG plant is located in Soyo, a former fishing town with one hotel and one decent restaurant roughly 200 miles away from the nearest large potential gas demanding city of Luanda, Angola's capital, means that the Angolan Energy Ministry are not planning for the facility to be the first step of construction in the development of an internal gas market. Officially the government claim that locating the LNG facility in Soyo is meant to kick start the region and make it a second centre of commerce; in reality, the city has stayed the same with the building site for the LNG plant and the pre-existing onshore infrastructure of the Kwanda oil field providing most of the jobs and life in Soyo. It seems likely that natural gas is, for Angola, a purely internationally-driven profit making industry and that the Angolan population will not be given access to most of the gas its own fields produce for heating and energy. With good reason, too: the region's current 2010 level of production – 219.5 billion cubic metres (bcm) in a year – will increase by nearly a third to over 305 billion cubic metres (bcm) by 2014, according to forecasts.[121] That simply equals far too much potential profit to be made by selling off rights to foreign companies for personal bungs, then profiting once more by selling on the energy produced.

In compensation for the unfair regime being fostered under President Dos Santos, some international companies are undertaking extremely active CSR movements in an attempt to curry the local populations' favour, and go some way to mitigate the backlash from the international community in supporting such a corrupt and unfair dictatorship as Dos Santos'. Total SA announced on 1 December 2010[122] – World AIDS Day – that they would be instigating an HIV/AIDS awareness programme in the communities their work touches; at the same time Chinese investors in the region from the China International Trust and Investment Corporation (CITIC) relayed to the press[123] news that they would begin construction on a new-build town in Ndalatando in the new year in co-operation with Sonangol. The near-3,000 houses in 210 hectares of land would provide accommodation for locals and is seen as mostly a goodwill gesture. CITIC are piggybacking on the government's plan to build a million houses by 2012, using community projects as an attempt to win onside residents that are quietly angry at government for placing their resources in the hands of the biggest international bidder. Various Chinese investors have repaired rail links, built football stadia (four brand new ones were erected in time for Angola to hold the 2010 African Cup of

Nations) and are looking to finance a state-of-the-art international airport to service the capital city of Luanda.

As discussed in the previous chapter, and with special attention because of the strength of dictatorship that Angola struggles under, the difficulty comes in drawing the line as to where community projects become implicit bribery of government. There is a strong argument that any payment – even if it benefits the community, rather than the individual politicians in charge of communities – is an attempt to silence opposition to prospective drilling. An exchange of goods is being offered: it is, in many ways, still cash for access (though the cash is used for the benefit of the many rather than the benefit of the few). Such investment in community projects is regularly used in the west, and not tainted with the notion of bribery. In reality, there is little difference between the historical (and sadly still current) African way of doing things where bribes are paid directly to local leaders and government officials, and the typical, acceptable western way of carrying out projects where similar amounts of money are placed into community projects. Opinions are still being bought, and money is being exchanged for the ability to siphon off gas and oil. Governments in many African nations, including those under Presidents Dos Santos in Angola, Jonathan in Nigeria and Obiang in Equatorial Guinea see less of a distinction between implicit and explicit bribery than those in the west; the line to them is much more blurred than to us.

One thing is for sure: in Angola and Equatorial Guinea, the profits from the oil and gas reserves they hold underground do not trickle down to the general populace in any meaningful way, bribes or no bribes. Ordinary Angolans "say their oil incomes have not had any effect on them materially[,] that poverty is still widespread and the country is almost taken over by the Chinese," report Ghanaian journalists.[124] Equatoguineans "live in abject poverty" and "do not feel the huge oil income materially. Equatorial Guinea's oil revenues in the 1980s have created one of the most supposedly wealthy and at the same time one of the most fraudulent regimes in the world." As with any number of African petrostates, the prevailing attitudes on the continent towards fraud, democracy and corruption mean that the rich get richer and the poor poorer from the proceeds of any oil and gas exploration.

*　　*　　*

International oil and gas companies have in the past paid money directly to Equatorial Guinea's President Obiang and his family: ExxonMobil, in a letter to Human Rights Watch, explained that "the practical realities of doing business in developing countries are challenging. E[quatorial] G[uinea], like many developing nations, has a limited number of local businesses and a small population of educated citizens. As a result, there is a small community of government officials and business owners. Not unexpectedly, many of these persons are connected by a network of social and family relations."[125] Marathon personally paid Obiang $2 million for the title to land near its Alba field in 2002 to expand its infrastructure and build new plants. There is no indication that Marathon paid above market price for the land, but it did go directly into the pocket of the President. Worse still, Hess paid $445,800 to lease a building from a relative of President Obiang in 2000. The relative was born in 1986. Hess paid nearly half a million dollars for the (now-lapsed) lease of a property to a 14-year old boy.

Equatorial Guinea stands to benefit greatly from its impending entry into the Community of Portuguese Language Countries (CPLC) in 2012[126], where it currently enjoys observer status. President Obiang is looking to take the country into the group to attempt to leverage new markets in Brazil for Equatoguinean natural gas and oil. This is an unabashed return headlong into the days of colonialism, with Obiang prepared to cede the entire linguistic makeup of the nation in order to assure entry to the CPLC. He is willing to make Portuguese the third official language of Equatorial Guinea, and return the country to the bosom of its colonial master from the 15th to 18th century, before it was pawned off to Spanish subjugation. With such a large potential payload to come into Obiang's hands from the Gulf of Guinea upon the arrival of a comprehensive geological survey, he is keen to make moves to allow him to offload the vast reserves of resources to strong demand markets for the benefit of himself and his closest advisers. There is a frenzied atmosphere akin to that of a high-rate auction room, where countries are throwing significant (though significantly *less* than would be paid for similar access in other neighbouring states) amounts of money towards President Obiang in attempt to gain access to the enormous amount of hydrocarbons that sit in his country's waters. China, Brazil and the world's other large economies are outbidding each other directly to the President who holds the gavel: currently the US is winning the bidding war, ploughing $7 billion into the Equatorial Guinea economy in 2010 to keep the gas and oil flowing.

Obiang welcomes it freely, and sees that little of it is given to the people who live closest to the production fields and feel the disruption and injustice of their natural resources being taken from them the most. The majority of the companies subcontracted by the Equatoguinean government to work with international companies are owned by Obiang's relations and cabinet partners – though officially the proportion of government earnings from the hydrocarbon contracts it signs with international companies is much lower than most other African nations: between 15 and 40%, where the average is somewhere between 45 and 90%. Obiang and his allies are out to make quick money, rather than the enormous potential amounts they could make from more favourable contracts. As long as there remains significant potential in Equatoguinean oil and gas, countries such as the US are willing to overlook governmental oversights and bad practice to ensure they are not left behind in one of the world's biggest potential boom areas. The United States had left the country in 1995 following some of the worst abuses against the average Equatoguineans, washing its hands of the nation's oil and gas potential. However it returned under the Presidency of George W Bush thanks to "intensive lobbying"[127] by American oil companies. The fear of China's looming presence on the continent stoked America's competitive nature once more, allowing it to put the need for a constant cheap oil supply above the human rights of Equatoguineans.

Colonialism runs rampant even in the potential coups that have occurred under Obiang's presidency: twelve serious attempts have been made at ousting the dictator in his 30 years of rule.[128] Perhaps the most well known to British eyes and ears is the failed coup roused by Mark Thatcher, son of former Prime Minister Margaret Thatcher, and his associate Simon Mann. Another conspirator, South African Nick du Toit was abundantly clear as to the reasoning behind the coup when compelled by the courts to produce a truthful statement. "This whole thing is about money," du Toit wrote. "Oil was the motivation behind the attempted coup." In Equatorial Guinea and Africa as a whole the news that two Britons, Mann and Thatcher, were complicit in the plot engendered fears that once again the colonial spirit was endemic in former imperial nations. The Equatorial Guinea Attorney General called "on the population to be vigilant with foreigners, regardless of colour, because the[ir] target is the wealth of Equatorial Guinea, the oil." Curiously President Obiang was less fearful than most, possibly buoyed by the assurance that of twelve coups not one had separated him from the lucrative spoils of his hydrocarbon assets. Though Thatcher and 82 other conspirators (including Simon Mann) plotted to kidnap or kill him in 2004, Obiang pardoned Mann in November 2009. This is because ultimately, Obiang had won. Equatoguineans who have previously attempted to overthrow the President in an attempt to better distribute the revenues from oil and gas reserves in the country have not been treated so leniently. President Obiang is often seen to be one of the more dangerous dictators in Africa, if not the world: a memorable line from The Independent's profile on him is that he "make[s] Robert Mugabe seem stable and benign."[129] Rumours run rife that Obiang eats the brain and testicles of his most hated opponents – rumours which far from being played down by Obiang, are amplified. The reason why the average Equatoguinean does not protest his lot more loudly is because of the cult of fear that Obiang has cultivated around himself. The state-owned and run radio station broadcast in July 2003[130] that Obiang "can decide to kill without anyone calling him to account and going to hell because it is God himself with whom he is in permanent contact", perpetuating the myths around this fearsome leader.

Obiang deposed his uncle, who had already established strict and uncompromising rule over Equatorial Guinea more than 30 years ago and built on the precedent established. A two-level inter-tribe power system between the Bantu people who make up the majority of the population has resulted in systemic discrimination. The Fang tribe, whose members make up more than four-fifths of the population of Equatorial Guinea (and an even larger proportion of the government) hold sway over the Bubi tribe, who are treated as second-class citizens.

The single fair and free election held in Equatorial Guinea was the local and municipal election, held across thirty districts in September 1995. Of the nineteen town halls where opposition parties won the public vote, only nine opposition candidates were allowed to take their seats: the government refuted the other ten opposition victories (though with false evidence) and kept their own candidates in power. It was the last time Obiang would dally with a democratic vote, and a democratic press too: Equatorial Guinea is the 12th most-censored country in the world by one estimate, placing it 45 places higher than Robert Mugabe's Zimbabwe.[131] Most news that makes it out of the country beyond that reported by state-owned media is a week or more old. EITI, the Extractive

Industries Transparency Intiative initially welcomed Equatorial Guinea to apply for EITI member status; having not received sufficient evidence of transparency or fairness, and following a lack of co-operation from Obiang's government, the EITI board announced in a personal letter to President Obiang of April 2010 that "Equatorial Guinea is [...] no longer considered an EITI implementing country."[132]

Obiang courted controversy in the west when he created the UNESCO-Obiang Nguema Mbasogo International Prize for Research in the Life Sciences in 2008 with a $3 million stipend. The winner of the prize (due to be awarded in 2010) would have received $300,000 but a concerted effort by human rights pressure organisations ensured that the prize – for scientific research based around "improving the quality of life" – was withdrawn by the UN in October 2010. Human rights campaigners found the concept of a President known for the systemic maltreatment of his people sponsoring a prize for improving the quality of life too galling.

The epigraph to this chapter shows that the distance between Equatorial Guinea law and western law and Equatoguinean and western morality is enormous, but this can be extrapolated (though possibly not quite as callously and casually as President Obiang's son and Forestry Minister Teodorin presents it) to the rest of Africa. ExxonMobil's letter to Human Rights Watch is also notable because perhaps more than any other group, it acknowledges that the situation in Africa is neither perfect nor hopeless. Currently – and the key word is currently – there are a small group of related or friendly people who control everything in the country, as there are at the heads of many African states. Currently these people must be appeased as they are the controllers of access to hydrocarbon basins and planning committees, but they must not monopolise western attention or money. There is a strong underbelly of everyday Africans who have the potential to rise above their current station and overthrow the current corrupt regimes and install a new, democratic ideal – but it takes time and development. Some have managed to get to that stage, and some are transitioning from expedient dictatorship to expedient democracy, having already moved on from dictatorship for the sake of dictatorship. The fear is that companies continue to prop up the dictators without helping the average African, ascribing to the colonial celebratist mindset. There is also a danger in taking the opposing view of the colonial apologist and leaving the unrepresented majority to battle for their own rights. Rather ExxonMobil's letter acknowledges that the best path forward is to try and engage with governments *and* people together, being mindful of the past *and* the unique present situation in which many African nations find themselves. In countries like Equatorial Guinea, where the dictatorship and biased government are more entrenched than others, this can prove difficult – but if drilling companies were to continue current practices then there would be no impetus for change in ruling style. Likewise, if they were to wash their hands of the country then the little proportion of oil and gas money that does benefit the general populace would disappear, and the rulers such as President Obiang would likely take out their anger on the people. Mediation then is the answer, alongside moderation, as is the case when dealing with most African countries.

The sad fact is that because of Equatorial Guinea's small population and large potential and realised reserves of oil and gas, were revenues distributed evenly its people would be amongst the very richest in the world: by GDP per capita the country stands, at $36,600, higher than the United Kingdom ($35,200), Spain ($33,700) and Germany ($34,100).[133] The country is one of only four in Africa whose GDP per capita is above the world average of $10,500 (the others are Gabon, Botswana and Libya). As it is more than three-quarters of the population live below the poverty line.[134]

Angola is in a similarly impoverished situation: lurching out of civil war, 2006 estimates[135] placed more than 40% of the population below the poverty line. President Dos Santos has made superficial concessions to the world (in order to gain $1.4 billion of pity money from the International Monetary Fund (IMF) in November 2009) by publishing accounts of revenue stemming from oil and gas production and condemning government corruption, but ultimately the system of self-interest remains. One telling factor is that while the Angolan government are happy to publish their own production figures on a government website, they are not interested in joining the Extractive Industries Transparency Initiative (EITI). At the same time as professing a new open society, Dos Santos pushed a new constitution through parliament in January 2010 that removes the concept of elected Presidents and allows the President two five-year terms beginning in 2012, meaning that by 2022 Dos Santos could have been in uninterrupted power as President of Angola for 43 years. For the international oil and gas community, the President is the person through whom access to Angolan hydrocarbons is granted for the foreseeable future.

The lack of transparency is a problem for Angolan oil and gas, with Sonangol's audited financial figures not being released publicly, despite one of the conditions of the IMF's 2009 payment being a free display of Sonangol's finances. There has been a continuing and consistent level of financial impropriety, found Human Rights Watch, since one of its first studies into the country discovered that Sonangol underpaid the Angolan Central Bank by more than $2.1 billion.[136] These possible financial misdeeds concern western governments and drilling companies, but the Chinese government and its state-owned exploration and production companies are much more forgiving of financial impropriety. The China International Fund (CIF) gave $2.9 billion to Angola in 2005 to help rebuild the country in the aftermath of the civil war through an intermediary company, the Reconstruction Office of Angola (GRN), which is under the direct control of Dos Santos. The benefits of easier access to hydrocarbons by getting in on the ground floor of Angolan redevelopment are clear: Chatham House reported that the "CIF seems to have successfully positioned itself between the Chinese and Angolan governments (and between Sonangol and Sinopec) and controls access to Angolan resources."[137] The economic benefits to China for this initial investment are huge: it has first refusal on access to the country's vast hydrocarbon resources and has built up the impression of being a world away from the domineering, imperialistic colonial powers of the west.

Some western companies are looking to roll back their investment in the country because of the questionable financial and ethical climate. ExxonMobil, who own a 25% stake in Angola's offshore block 31 – which will produce between 150,000 and 300,000 barrels of oil a day when production begins in 2012 – were looking to sell up their share in the field in late 2010. Extracting themselves from block 31 resulted in a severe downsizing of ExxonMobil assets in Angola, as the company only operated four blocks in the country. Total SA, who also own a part of block 31, were looking to exit too, despite the promising production predictions. In their place Sonangol courted India's Oil & Natural Gas Corporation, who were willing to pay almost $2 billion for the lucrative stake in the field. Other Indian companies have sought out assets in Ghana and Nigeria, as well as other African nations, in an attempt to match the increasing oil and gas demand within their country. They are being treated preferentially by African officials and state-owned gas and oil companies because of their thriving economies and their shared colonial history.

An Indian hydrocarbon company would know full well the experience of living under colonial rule, Africans recognise, and they would be less likely to exploit the continent unfairly, they believe. China is similar, they posit, in that they have lived for decades under a cloud of perceived inferiority promoted by the west. However both Asian superpowers' supreme economic growth has not come through lax business dealings: they are careful, cost-aware economies that look to drive beneficial deals as aggressively as their western counterparts. Yet still Angola is hugely close to China – a closeness which is only increasing. In September 2010 Angola was the second largest oil exporter to China, only 0.1% behind the oil producing giant that is Saudi Arabia. In all, Angola accounts for 17.4% of China's crude imports,[138] and looks set to continue to provide the Asian superpower with a large amount of crude oil. The west has become too complacent in believing that its laissez faire and haughty attitude is enough to continue to be assured of African resource supplies. Jean Ping struck a defiant note while sitting next to the EU's Jose Manuel Barroso at a press conference in Tripoli in November 2010. "Africa has already begun to diversify its strategic partners," he said. "The world has today realised that it will be increasingly difficult – and even impossible – to continue to systematically overlook an entire continent with 53 of the 192 member states of the UN; a continent on which 1 billion consumers live, and whose surface area is 10 times the size of Europe as well as India [...] a continent with considerable resources and with one of the largest reservoirs of raw materials on the planet – which places it at the centre of the global issues."[139] China, Japan and India – three of the emerging main export markets for African gas and oil – have been paying Africa the attention it demands and are willing to support its development, meaning they have been given first preference on the vast amounts of hydrocarbons the continent is exporting via LNG and oil tankers.

Divided nations

"The white man is very clever. He came quietly with his religion. We were amused at his foolishness and allowed him to stay. Now he has won our brothers, and our clan can no longer act like one. He has put a knife on the things that held us together and we have fallen apart."

– Chinua Achebe, *Things Fall Apart*

The Berlin Conference held in 1884 was a grand meeting of old imperial hands. *Chargés d'affaires* from Europe's leading colonial powers gathered in long drawing rooms to sit around impossibly large tables, a phalanx of wallflower advisors backing them, in order that they might better organise their individual stakes to parts of Africa. A great map of Africa was hung from one of the rooms' high ceilings, matching the huge heavy curtains for weight and splendour. This was the great theoretical carve-up of Africa into neat geometric lines and right angles: "you can try your luck at taming the savages in this bit as long as you leave us this and this", they would discuss between breaks.

Called by King Leopold II at his luxurious Berlin villa, the conference brought together representatives from the United Kingdom, the Ottoman Empire, Austria-Hungary, Sweden-Norway, Spain, Denmark, France, Belgium, Italy, Russia and Portugal to work out an African policy when it came to geographical claims. All turned up. The United States were offered a seat at the table, but chose not to attend. They talked over several months and came up with the General Act of the Berlin Conference, a diktat which outlined in international (colonial) law each individual nation's claims to parts of Africa and the all-important shipping routes which would allow their interests in the continent to flourish. When the representations took their seats in the panelled walled rooms of Leopold's villa, 80% of Africa still remained under tribal control. 18 years later, in 1902, 90% of it was officially European-owned.

The Berlin Conference codified countries' rights to claim land which was not really theirs: it established arbitrary territories in which they could contest ownership, which in turn led to the arbitrary borders that each power established for the colonies they created. Had either level of cartography been more compassionate and less focused on straight lines and 90 degree angles, some of the current complications that seem endemic in African nations might today be avoided.

We have already seen just how divided nations can be through the case of Nigeria and its government's tempestuous relationship with the people of the Niger Delta. While the seat of power lies firmly in the urban north of the country, most of the hydrocarbon reserves (and consequently most of the potential economic prosperity) lies in the south's backwaters, amongst the deeply tribal, deeply proud residents of the Niger Delta. Although Britain and the United States have struggled with a strong north-south divide in their past, each country has managed to move beyond geographical division and become united; many African nations have yet to do so.

The problem is one of temperament, with the north and south often being divided by simply more than basic geography. Usually there is a difference in way of life, with the often more rural and agrarian, traditional half of a nation often sitting on the overwhelming majority of the reserves. Sometimes the division is exacerbated by a religious divide, often stemming back thousands of years. The gap between the two people becomes intractable, and a strong sense of 'us versus them' – or to use a postcolonial term, 'us' and 'the Other', exists.

Up to 9 January 2011 Sudan was still nominally a single country. The largest in Africa, Sudan could never claim to be united. Since its independence from the shackles of joint colonialism from Egypt and Britain in 1956, the country has often dominated western newspapers and television bulletins for the prolonged and particularly bloody civil war ("the most protracted conflict in Africa,"[140] Sudanese Ambassador to the UN Daffa-Alla Elhay Ali Osman said morosely on the eve of South Sudanese secession) that has existed for decades. The country has been blighted by genocide and resultant famine in Darfur that has produced some of the most harrowing images of the 20th and 21st century. On 9 January the already politically autonomous people of Southern Sudan, who gained semi-independence from the north as part of the détente which closed the civil conflict, began voting to be fully independent of its northern neighbours, in large part so that they did not have to funnel the majority of their profit from the extensive petroleum reserves that exist mostly in south Sudan to the northern government in Khartoum. They queued for hours in the heat and in the sand on the first day (despite polls being open for a full week), wearing their best clothes, to place an inky thumbprint next to a picture of clasped hands – for remaining tied to the northern government – or a solitary, defiant open hand raised high to signify they were adding theirs to the list of names who wanted to secede from Khartoum. Hordes of international journalists and observers came to cities across Sudan – including the future South Sudanese capital Juba – to see the historic referendum take place. The poll brought together Ghana's former UN Secretary-General Kofi Annan, former US President Jimmy Carter and perhaps most puzzlingly actor George Clooney to observe and confer on the voting process legitimacy that it was fair and free. Barack Obama wrote an editorial in the *New York Times* the day before the referendum, highlighting to the world just how great a step the referendum on secession was. "It will have consequences not only for Sudan, but also for sub-Saharan Africa and the world," the President wrote. "The world is watching, united in its determination to make sure that all parties in Sudan live up to their obligations. [...] A successful vote will be cause for celebration and an inspiring step forward in Africa's long journey toward democracy and justice." The vote was hugely important (opinions on the matter were so strong and voters so keen to express their viewpoint that before the start of the fourth day of voting officials already announced that the 60% turnout threshold required to ratify the vote had been passed by some distance) and held massive implications for both the Sudan that remained and the new South Sudan that was created as a result of the will of the people.

The region holds by most estimates more than 80% of all Sudanese oil reserves, and the share of revenues ($8 billion from 2004-10) that the south is left with after splitting it with the government in Khartoum is responsible for a staggering 98% of southern Sudan's entire budget.[141]

Though that is an enormous amount for a country where 9 million of 10 million southern Sudanese live on less than a single dollar a day, the informal nature of the split between the south and north of Sudan meant that the autonomous southern government held back on spending its oil revenue on roads, hospitals and schools in favour of keeping its weapons stocks high in case the north decided to encroach on its natural resource lifeline. Now that the split has been codified, and Sudan is no longer a nation divided but two separate countries, the southern Sudanese government have promised strong spending on infrastructure designed to improve the quality of life in the world's newest – and one of its poorest – countries. The south will still be reliant on the north, however, until they build their own refining and export facilities as the pipeline system that transports the oil from the south to refineries and export terminals runs through the north of the country, under the jurisdiction of Khartoum's government.

David Loro, the Undersecretary at the southern Sudanese Energy Ministry had outlined[142] before the referendum on secession that were the south to break away from the north it would rapidly build its own refineries and export facilities to sever all ties with the Khartoum government, and gain back the billions of dollars it was forced to share under a single Sudan. The $1.8 billion Warrap refinery in the south will be able to deal with 50,000 barrels per day when it is built and comes online in 2014. For its part, the north was equally willing to make a clean break from the south, and to leave them their oil reserves. Before the secession vote, President Omar al-Bashir said "if they choose unity, we are ready for the national government to give up its full share in the oil of the south to the government of the south."[143]

So vital was the issue of oil to the secession that the two previously warring armies – the Sudan People's Liberation

Army (SPLA) and the Sudan Armed Forces (SAF) – as well as the south Sudanese police force and the National Intelligence and Security Services, joined together to form a taskforce focused on ensuring the continued safety and smooth running of the hydrocarbon sector throughout the difficult referendum period. Sudan's division is ostensibly about hydrocarbons and the distribution of revenue, but that is simply a modern excuse for a centuries-old conflict. Like a large number of other African nations, the division is tribal, political and religious. The north of Sudan is mainly Muslim – much like Nigeria – and traces its lineage back to Arabian forebears. The northern Arabs, as in Mauritania, managed to gain the most power and established a capital, a government and a sense of power over the south. Southern Sudan, now an independent nation, was for years forced into semi-subservience to its northern neighbours because of its dominant religions – Animism and Christianity – and the fact that the majority of its population are black Africans. The north instilled the Arabic language into the south alongside the other official language of the state, the colonial English, and the tribal languages that flourished in the south were forced to be used as local cant rather than the dominant language of tribal relations that they had been for hundreds of years.

Once again the blame for deep divisions in Sudan can be laid at the feet of Britain. Lord Kitchener quelled Sudanese nationalists in the late years of the 19th century by might, and then installed an Egyptian yes man as Governor-General of the state. By 1924 the British colonisers recognised the religious divisions in the country, but rather than choosing to mediate between Muslim and Christian/Animist representatives they chose to divide the country into two territories, each with their own ruler and religion. This was not an empty division of territory: it was mandated by the British that northerners could not travel south, nor could southerners travel north. Isolated and left to their own practices, separate identities were engendered which made reconciling the country when it eventually gained independence nigh-on impossible. Successive Presidents since independence calcified the north's stranglehold on the south by imposing tenets of sharia law onto the national legal system and turning Sudan into a haven for fundamentalists and terrorists. Only through the extensive conflict – all of which can be traced back to British queasiness at facing the problem of religious tension – and prolific bloodshed of prolonged civil war did the north and south manage to thrash out an agreement in 2005 which led to the eventual secession of the south and establishment of a totally non-dependent North and South Sudan. President Obama spoke of the problems of a divided nation thanks to colonial casualness when establishing and maintaining borders in Ghana in mid-2009. It is easy to blame colonialism, he said. "Yes, a colonial map that made little sense bred conflict, and the west has often approached Africa as a patron, rather than a partner."[144]

It is this sense of condescension – that Africa is a patron, to be patronised (in both its literal and more loaded meaning) – which has proved most damaging to international companies. Somehow there is a strain of common cultural thought in the west that belies rational thinking. Though most know and acknowledge that the colonial past we subjected African nations to was horrifically wrong, subconsciously the thought still exists that because in the past we had this particular approach (of Africa as patron), we should refigure our current relationship with Africa in the same way. Doing so only breeds divisions between Africa and the west, and within Africa itself. It is equally damaging still, throwing African gas and oil interests into the hands of competing markets. The Chinese National Petroleum Corporation (CNPC) stand to remain the beneficiary of this western patronising stance on Africa, with the world's newest country pledging to honour the contracts – which comprised China's first forays into Africa some 16 years ago, in 1995 – that dictate 60% of Sudan's oil exports must be loaded on a slow boat to China. Through division there is one common bond that holds nations together: a distrust of the west and a belief that under current arrangements and given current attitudes towards Africa, making deals with the likes of the UK, France and the USA is a last resort when China or India cannot or have not stepped in.

Dutch MP Sharon Gesthuizen travelled to Nigeria with a small delegation in late 2010 in order to better investigate the effect Dutch company Shell was having on the Niger Delta and its people, and whether there was basis to the fact that Nigeria is a divided nation – between rich and poor, capital city and Niger Delta – because of the oil revenue the marshlands of the Delta produce. She landed in Lagos a week before Christmas in the fug of "an oppressive heat."[145] She was asked almost immediately at her first press conference, held in the hotel she was staying at in the Nigerian capital, why it had taken so long for a foreign politician to involve themselves in the Delta. "That is hard to explain," she said – and subsequently wrote for Dutch daily SP.

> In recent years I've noticed several ministers and secretaries of state were less than willing to comment about what's going on. Is it because it's difficult to talk about the situation in a country where corruption plays such a key role? Or is it also an unwillingness to bring Shell into disrepute? Nigeria has a long way to go before it can be classed as a developed country. There is hardly an electricity network – most of it comes from generators – and there is no running water in most places.
>
> The streets of Lagos are like most others: poor people of all trades desperately trying to earn a daily crust. Nigeria doesn't really have tourism. It's said to be too dangerous. Militias in the south of the country actively plot against the oil companies, and the chance of being robbed – or kidnapped – is very real. In

addition internet crime, including phishing, gives Nigeria a bad name.

Yet the Niger Delta is so resource-rich. There is so much oil in the ground that not only Dutch companies, but French, Canadian, American and other companies set up camp here. Unfortunately doing so affects the Delta people's land, water and air with pollution, making normal life impossible in the Delta. Where does the money go? The companies take their gains, obviously, but the top layer of the Nigeria people will be better off too [through bribes]. By the Wikileaked documents [alleging high-level corruption] we learned where the money goes.

Her dispatches proved insightful, showing the disconnect between rich and poor in Nigeria, and how it has divided a nation in approach to foreign companies. The second and third articles spoke truth to power:

Sunday morning I met with Mutiu Sunmonu, Managing National Director of Shell Nigeria. His first reply to my questions about the attitude of Shell and the problems resultant in the Niger Delta was that the people themselves must take responsibility for their situation. That sounds great, but is easier said than done when you have no income, no home, no land and few rights to boot.

At the highest level here, people are bought. […]

The question that every company that works here asks themselves is: Do I participate in that system or do I fight against it? Contributing to it basically means bolstering the vicious circle, making the wound deeper. And trying to divide and conquer is worse. Make one villager a millionaire so he'll defend your interests, and you turn the rest against you. The seed of discontent has been sown. The village – which can be used together to fight for the common good – becomes a site of internal strife. [...]

Joining in the corruption is easier; it's cheaper to keep on polluting, too. But Mutiu is right: every Nigerian should stop asking and waiting, and should take responsibility. Set a good example by your actions, and the rest will follow.[146]

[...] It's clear what's happened. A small sliver – the upper crust – of the Nigerian people steal anything they can and don't leave the poverty-stricken Nigerians they are supposed to represent a stitch. The population of the state gets nothing: no schools, no hospitals, hardly any roads.[147]

The precise same thing that Gesthuizen wrote about in Nigeria has happened in a raft of other African nations. In Mauritania, Angola and Equatorial Guinea the divide between rich and poor is blatant, and is so ingrained in the national psyche that the people have become almost too weary to fight against the leadership. In Nigeria the problems remain, and are gradually compounding – "no schools, no hospitals, hardly any roads" is very much endemic of the situation in some parts of the Niger Delta. Ghanaians are fearful of the same thing happening, and are fighting vociferously to remind their government not to fall into the trap that so many other nations have done, wooed by the promise of power and money from hydrocarbon resources.

It is in the interest of western companies to prevent the promulgation of this class division based purely on power held, rather than merit. This was not the case in pre-secession Sudan, where "persistent calls for clear and transparent information on [the country's] oil revenues" have even now yet to yield satisfactory information."[148] Rather, the deep division over power was and still is further entrenched by corruption in the highest echelons. The report by Global Witness on Sudanese oil revenues found that neither side was free of culpability for cooking their books: the Sudanese government and the main company operating in Sudan – the China National Petroleum Corporation (CNPC), who by most estimates are credited with at least a 60% hold on all oil produced in the country[149] – each differed in their production figures, by up to a quarter of the entire total. Both blamed the other for trying to pull the wool over the public's eyes: the government said that the CNPC measured the large amounts of water and associated gas (neither of which is an industry standard) to 'overinflate' figures (the reality is that the north-based government were keen to underplay the amount of oil produced in order to sidestep the meatier payments of oil revenue to the south Sudanese government) while the CNPC claimed that they use up between 5 and 15% of the entire payload of oil in refining and transporting it (again, an amount that is baffling to most industry players). What is happening is top-scraping of oil revenue and deliberate under reporting of production figures so that those in control of the resource can surreptitiously gain while the average Sudanese citizen is being left out of the benefits of oil revenue. That this was the case even before the south Sudanese referendum indicates just how bad an agent oil and gas revenue can be in dividing nations.

All this comes to harm the average man, woman and child in African nations. Aside from their country being torn asunder by religious, class and caste warfare, they must also contend with the results of such divisions. By both sides of the Sudanese argument – the north government and the CNPC –

falsifying figures, no-one knows the true value of the resource that sits beneath Sudanese land. This means that no-one can truly capitalise on the actual worth of that resource, and make the most of it. Both sides were – and are – living in a world of fantasy and made-up figures, and are very likely underestimating the amount of gas and oil which is available to produce, market and sell to international markets. If they truly knew the level of hydrocarbons that Sudan (and now the completely independent country of South Sudan) was sitting on, they would be able to better establish an infrastructure to exploit positively the huge, potentially life-changing amount of oil and gas which is available to them.

For western nations to stand idly by and worse, to abet such divisions is hugely discouraging and leaves an indelible negative mark on the globe's collective consciousness. However again a balance must be struck so as not to fall into the remarkably easy western approach of infantilising Africa as a continent, and pretending that it must be mollycoddled because of a sense of its racial inferiority. To meddle in a problem which Africans acknowledge and are making steps towards remedying is to believe that for some reason Africans are any different to those in the west. For too long the prevailing view has been that Africa is 'the Other': the west suffers a collective cultural amnesia about the same sort of deep-rooted divisions that plague many African nations. You too have your own problems, those who believe the west are too eager to put their nose in other people's business would point out, and you haven't yet sorted them out.

Conclusion

"The state of Africa is a scar on the conscience of the world."

– Tony Blair, speech to Labour Part
Conference, 2 October 2001

Blair's successor as Prime Minister Gordon Brown left Downing Street on 11 May 2010 holding the hands of his two sons and with his wife, Sarah. "Fraser", his youngest son, "skipped away", said Brown in an interview[150] with *The Guardian*. As the ministerial car exited Downing Street, Brown claimed he was retiring to the life of a backbench MP in Kirkcaldy and Fife, taking up the most important job any man could hold: that of "a husband and a father." His first international speaking engagement after stepping out of office was in sunny Kampala, Uganda more than two months later, addressing African leaders at the fifteenth African Union Summit.

He spoke eloquently of the same themes which run through this book: the need to not be a colonial celebratist or apologist, but to engage with Africa on equal terms to ensure its development and growth. His speech on 24 July[151] was listened to by the Presidents and Prime Ministers of African nations, and contained the following truths and goals:

> Since the turn of the Millennium we have witnessed a decade of development, but have thought too narrowly of development as aid. In the coming decade we need to go well beyond an old paradigm of development based on relationships of donor and recipient, and adopt instead a new conception of development as a partnership for investment and growth. The future is no longer giving and receiving, but instead investing together in a future which is shared. [...]
>
> No injustice should endure forever and it is to your credit as leaders that you as a group have achieved more for social justice by working together in these last two decades than has been achieved in the previous 100 years.

But as Nelson Mandela has said – the struggle for justice never ceases, and once one mountain top has been scaled, you always see a new summit to climb towards.

And my argument today is that while Africa's achievements – your achievements – are enormous, the world asks yet more from you now.

Africans have always inspired progressives with the heroism of your struggle – against the wrongs of imperialism, against apartheid, against poverty. But it is time not merely to inspire us, but to lead us.

Africa must lead, because today, because of the interdependence of our economies, and because what happens in the richest city of richest country can directly affect the poorest citizen in the poorest country, we can no longer think of policies as only for the North or only for the South, or only for developed countries or only for developing countries: shared global problems require shared global solutions. […]

I believe the key imperative for the world – not just for Africa – is delivering for this continent not just what we have seen these last 10 years – a decade of growth – but something much more than that. What I believe is possible is a continuous uninterrupted period of 3 decades of growth. This should not be a sprint for growth but a marathon of growth. […]

And so the world needs a new driver of consumer demand, a new market, and a new dynamo. In short; the world needs Africa. Some time ago we moved beyond the idea of charity, and said that Africa's development was not about charity but about justice. But the imperative is stronger still; it is both about justice and our shared prosperity. There is, quite simply, no sustainable route back to long term prosperity in Bonn and Boston and Bristol, without growth in Accra and Addis and Abuja [...] people are now rightly talking not just of East Asian tigers, but of African lions. [...]

Of course the creation of wealth and an increase in trade will not, in and of themselves, equal development. Prosperity does not simply trickle down but must be actively distributed to ensure that the many and not just the few see the benefit. But there is no sustainable poverty reduction strategy which does not depend, in the end, on dynamic private and public sectors creating decent work. And so that must be our primary goal. [...]

African growth can only be sustained in tandem with a huge upswing in good governance. Companies simply will not invest without guarantees of minimum standards on corruption, stability of regulation, property rights and the rule of law. I know that this is at the heart of NEPAD's work, and I want to congratulate you on all the progress which has been made so far. And I truly believe that if that progress continues, and the ideas I have discussed today are adopted, that we stand at the beginning of a decade of investment, and the dawn of a global society.

We are at the beginning of the second decade of a still-young century. How the 21st century unfolds is in large part in the hands of the people on this room, and the leaders who meet in the coming days. My message to you is simple, and it is a message not simply from Britain, but from people all over the world. It is time to rise. Rise, because just as Africa needs the world, the world needs Africa.

Half the respondents to PwC's 2010 Oil & Gas Survey have claimed medium or significant difficulties in realising their growth strategy because of risks to the physical safety of their staff; 55% because of anti-competitive practices and two-thirds because of outright fraud. Until these three major problems are altered, Africa's potential to profit from hydrocarbon production and development will always be hamstrung in some way.

Additionally there are huge problems negotiating with countries where democracies are still struggling to find their feet. On one day alone in December 2010 came the news that elections in Egypt, Sudan and the Cote d'Ivoire had failed in some way. The Cote d'Ivoire electoral commission missed their deadline for announcing the results of a Presidential election, leading many to believe that the votes were being rigged and candidates to request that the results are annulled and the election rerun before first poll results were even able to be announced. The two candidates, incumbent Laurent Gbagbo and challenger Alassane Ouattra (who was declared winner of the vote by the country's electoral commission) both claimed to have won the vote and were both sworn in as President at different ceremonies. Sudan's troubled elections, scheduled for 9 January 2011, were put in doubt when it was revealed that the country was unable to organise an independent group to print ballots (the vote eventually went smoothly) and Egypt, one of Africa's most developed countries, saw rioting on the streets before results were announced over widespread accusations of fraud in an election where one party's candidates, the Muslim Brotherhood, have been forced to stand as independents for decades because of restrictions on religious political parties. The strident chants of student protestors in Tunisia and Algeria over government ineptitude chimed in the New Year as opposed to the west's fireworks and clock tower bells. Kenya's Industrialisation Minister, Henry Kogsey, resigned over corruption charges and the even more serious accusation of stoking violence in his country. Gabonese politicians secreted project funding in French banks – and placed it in their own purses at a later date – and two bomb attacks in Nigeria, one on New Year's Eve and one on Christmas Eve, killed more than 100 people trying to celebrate peace and goodwill to all men. Africa is still a troubled continent, for sure. But it has a bright future.

What Gordon Brown spoke of in his speech is the unmatched potential of Africa to drive the future of the world: "if we can agree a new model of post-crisis growth then Africa – already a $1.6 trillion economy – will continue to grow even faster than the rest of the world," he said in his speech. "This is not my assessment, but that of the world's leading companies and analysts." By way of comparison, Russia's economy is an equal amount, showing that with careful management Africa as a continent has the true potential to become a new global superpower.

The rise of China is clear on this continent, indicating they have seen the same data Gordon Brown had. As Deborah Brautigam wrote in January 2010's *Foreign Policy* magazine, "since 2004, China has concluded deals in at least seven resource-rich countries in Africa, for a total of nearly $14 billion. Reconstruction in war-battered Angola, for example, has been helped by three oil-backed loans from Beijing, under which Chinese companies have built roads, railways, hospitals, schools, and water systems. Nigeria took out two similar loans to finance projects that use gas to generate electricity. Chinese teams are building one hydropower project in the Republic of the Congo (to be repaid in oil) and another in Ghana (to be repaid in cocoa beans)."

She continues: "of course, China's loans pose some risks for the African recipients, particularly if Chinese firms are awarded infrastructure contracts without competitive bidding or if prices for the resources, the basis of the loan repayments, are fixed in advance. There is always a risk that African governments will not maintain infrastructure investments and that the Chinese projects' environmental and social safeguards will be too lax. Chinese construction companies often bring in Chinese manpower -- on average about 20 percent of the total labour their projects require -- reducing opportunities for Africans. When they do employ locals, Chinese firms often offer low wages and low labour standards." Still, Brautigam writes, "the terms of Chinese loans tend to be better than those of deals from Western companies."

For African nations, China is seen as the better of two evils. For a start, their blurring of the distinctions between aid and business loans, and between government and internationally-focused national oil companies, means that for African nations striking oil deals is tantamount to simultaneously striking up a close international governmental bond with the Chinese. To fall into co-operation with the likes of the CNPC or CNOOC is to also fall under the secure blanket of China on the international world, with all the assistance and backing that entails. In China, the government control the oil and gas companies; to do a deal with them is to do a deal with the government, and to expect partnership to extend far beyond purely the due diligence and care of hydrocarbons. International oil companies are used in China as another branch of the Foreign Ministry. There is still the real risk though that their terms of partnership are just as biased as those agreed with western companies. Currently in the corridors of power there is a blinkered approach to diplomacy and dealmaking with China and other Asian economies, believing that they simply must be operating from a more pleasing moral level than the European former colonialists that want to continue to capitalise on Africa's vast natural resources. They are more efficient with help than western former colonial powers, and Africans prefer their "no strings attached" deals with the continent.

The Kenyan Ambassador to China, Julius Ole Sunkuli, sat down for a lunch on 8 February 2010 with an American diplomat based in Beijing. Over their food the diplomat talked about the possibility of China joining western aid development programmes for Africa; Sunkuli reeled in horror. "Africa was better off," he said, "thanks to China's practical, bilateral approach to development assistance," according to the diplomat's report on the meeting in a cable to Washington. "Sunkuli said Africans were frustrated by western insistence on capacity building, which translated, in his eyes, into conferences and seminars. They instead preferred China's focus on infrastructure and tangible projects."[152]

In July 2007 French President Nicolas Sarkozy travelled to Dakar to give a speech on French history in Africa and the hope of restarting relations without the taint of colonialism[153]. His speech began well, acknowledging the past's impact on the present: "I did not come to erase the past, which can't be erased. I did not come to deny either the faults or the crimes, for there were faults and crime." He continued correctly that "Europeans came to Africa as conquerors. They took the land and your ancestors. They banned the gods, the languages, the beliefs, the customs of your fathers. They told your fathers what they should think, what they should believe, what they should do. They cut your fathers from their past, they stripped them of their souls and roots. They disenchanted Africa." However he then took a condescending tone, saying that the colonist "took but I want to say with respect that he also gave. He constructed bridges, roads, hospitals, dispensaries, schools. He rendered virgin land fertile, he gave his effort, his work, his knowledge. I want to say here that not all the colonists were thieves, not all the colonists were exploiters. Colonization is not responsible for all of Africa's current difficulties. It is not responsible for the bloody wars Africans carry out with each other. It is not responsible for the genocides. It is not responsible for the dictators. It is not responsible for fanaticism. It is not responsible for the corruption, for the lies. I have come to propose, to the youth of Africa, not to have you forget this tearing apart and this suffering, which cannot be forgotten, but to have you overcome and surpass them."

Africans' response to this was clear: rather than a resetting of French-African relations, this was a simultaneous perpetuation of the colonial past of Africans being responsible for their own problems and a belief that some beneficial aspects of colonialism can excuse the worst parts. France had already been tainted in some countries such as Angola, who in 2004 refused to renew licences in an offshore oil block for Total SA, instead giving the rights to the block to Sinopec, one of China's largest oil companies. Perhaps most worryingly, the *Financial Times* reported that "until recently many French companies still referred [as of January 2011] to the region as the *pré carré*, or 'backyard',"[154] a hangover from the colonial era when large swathes of Africa were the foreign summer retreats of the French aristocracy, who could enjoy different surroundings and 'strange looking people' with their quaint culture.

The problem is one of approach: former Shell chairman John Jennings has said in the past that "oil breeds arrogance because it's so powerful."[155] To many minds, the power that international oil and gas companies hold over countries manifests itself as arrogance across the negotiating table. In Africa – precisely because of the past of arrogant colonial powers controlling its subjects – that arrogance is poisonous to mutual goodwill.

The lure of power stemming from gas and oil does not only work on the western side of a negotiating table, however. Ugandan President Museveni took to the podium at the nation's 44th independence day celebrations in October 2006 and officially announced the discovery of oil in the country. Seeking to quieten fears that the new discovery could cause problems for the country, he stated "there is a lot of nonsense that the oil will be a curse. No way." Seeking his own reason for the multitude of countries that ascribe to the oil curse myth, he found the truth: "Oil becomes a curse when you have got useless leaders – and I can say we don't approach that description even by a thousandth of a mile."[156] It can become an alluring influence that allows politicians to negotiate on personally expedient terms rather than for the national good. A balance must be struck then in recognising that oil and gas corrupt on both sides, and that both sides realise it. There is therefore governmental hesitancy towards foreign companies when it comes to negotiations: they know that those they face across the table are looking for beneficial terms (very possibly at the expense of the government and its people) and that if they do not carefully negotiate terms to benefit their country and people that those same people will accuse them of corruption and self-interest. "An economy monolithically focused on oil and the revenues that flow from it"[157] is not a house formed on stable foundations in any sense of the term.

It is, of course, in the interests of the west and the world's security of supply for Africa to build stable governments and secure hydrocarbon laws. US Secretary of State Hillary Clinton spoke in Washington DC of the need to "encourage Nigeria, Angola, and other energy-producing countries to manage their resources and escape the natural resource curse that has plagued much of the continent. We believe that within the right legal framework Africa can be an enormous market for investment and for economic growth, as well as a secure producer and supplier of energy."[158] As to whether Africa chooses to look favourably on the west, its former colonial masters, or the rising economies of the east is yet to be seen. However one thing is clear: as Gordon Brown said in his first major public speech after office, "people are now rightly talking not just of East Asian tigers, but of African lions." Which side – whether Asia or the west – will be allowed in the lion's cage is down to individual approaches, and how willing each side are to move away from the tired colonial approaches which have typified the past several hundred years of African relations.

Epilogue: South Sudan

"I feel excited because we are going to be independent and that independence means we can think freely. I can think about my future and know that I can have a 10-year plan without fear that our political process will be interrupted by the northern government and all other forces that were limiting South Sudanese from thinking about their futures and their dreams."

– Wol Akujang, Sudanese civil war orphan, 13 January 2011

In the example of South Sudan there is a beacon of hope that Africa is eventually overcoming its inherent problems and moving away from a postcolonial fug which has for more than 50 years in some cases left it disorganised, disrupted and corrupted. The recognition that a divided nation should divide was an important moment of clarity and a step towards redressing the poor state of the arbitrary nations that those colonialists who met at a villa in Berlin in 1884 foisted upon Africa. European observers, who had for more than a century thought of Africa as a third-tier continent, rooted in the 'third world' in its most literal hierarchical sense, said that the South Sudanese referendum "was credible and well organised[,] free and peaceful."[159]

The petrostate's referendum on whether to split into two nations and give the world its newest country was an act of self-determinism which indicates the growing power and autonomy of Africa, and bodes well for the future of its oil and gas. Finally, after a long hangover from colonial past, we are seeing African lions rise to their full potential. Rather than the worst quasi-racist views of colonial celebratists being realised through in-fighting and bickering, South Sudan saw a legitimate and largely peaceful demonstration of democracy, returning a near-universal belief in secession. In Juba alone, 95% of voters turned out to vote and 96% of those wanted to split from Khartoum, according to Associated Press observations. Official figures told the story better than any highfalutin language ever could: 3,851,994 votes cast (3,837,406 of them valid), with 1.17% voting for unity and 98.83% voting for secession. In the ironically-named Unity region, 497,477 people voted for a split. Just 90 voted for unity.

The referendum was largely on the future of Sudan's large oil reserves, the high stakes and incredibly potential reserves of which mean that it is all the more incredible that the process has passed quite so smoothly to date. That this was achieved in a country where a 21-year civil war which accounted for more than 2 million deaths wrought apart Muslim and Christian was even more impressive. There will need to be co-operation between the now north Sudan and the new South Sudan, not least because they share borders but also because until South Sudan can establish a transport and pipeline infrastructure it must still use the existing Sudanese pipelines to transport the hydrocarbons which hold so much value in establishing its nascent economy. Ezekiel Lol Gatkuoth, Head of the South Sudan Mission to the US admitted as much when he said "we are basically [currently inter]dependent on the oil. The oil is in the south, the pipeline is going northwards. For us, we need the north – and the north needs us. We have relations with the north; indirectly the north will [still] benefit from the oil."[160]

Already South Sudan has struck deals with Total SA and Star Petroleum, a Spanish company, to explore blocks estimated to hold enough oil to treble current production. Petroleum Minister Garang Diing said that daily production could be ramped up by 2014 from its current rate of half a million barrels to two million or more barrels. And in a statement which proved hopeful for western oil companies, the new Minister indicated that the South Sudanese government would shy away from more alluring, but perhaps in the long term more harmful agreements with the more unscrupulous and less experienced Asian oil conglomerates. "We need to diversify [our] capital from some Asian [economies] – China, Malaysia and India especially – to get western experience, [who have] the best technologies and the best practices."[161] For a country which has broken off from the nation that provided China its first inroads into the African gas and oil world, this is a large step forward – and an equally significant step away from its northern former partner.

The stumbling blocks are there still. The Comprehensive Peace Agreement (CPA) between the north and the south of the then-united Sudan was signed in 2005; for six years the north largely obfuscated while the south tried to thrash out details of what would happen in the event that the planned referendum took place, and the people voted for secession. For one reason or another (and the reasons seem quite clear to most), the north did not brook any notion of what would happen once the people voted yes. That leaves the two sides until July 2011 to sort out a litany of problems which need to be agreed upon to ensure a clean break and a decent foundation for South Sudan to build upon. One of the most major of these is oil revenue and transportation – vital to both sides for providing the lion's share of their annual revenue and budget, and something which through accident or design is likely to keep Sudan and South Sudan chained to each other for a while yet.

Yet in self-determination comes the recognition that South Sudan is one of the first states in Africa to truly step away from all auspices of the old colonial way of life. In this newest country there are no ties whatsoever to an imperial or colonial past; no memories, formal or informal, which can give western former colonial powers some sort of leverage in negotiating access to the quantifiably vast oil reserves. There are likewise no colonial nightmares of the past with which to discourage South Sudanese officials or the people from doing business with the west for fear of lapsing into a second wave of colonialism, fuelled by the precious resource. South Sudan is writing a new history for itself on a totally blank page.

Many of the young South Sudanese who queued to vote for secession – putting their inky thumbprint next to the symbol of a raised, single hand – had until the days before the referendum never set foot in their homeland. They were born and raised in Khartoum or other northern countries, having been trapped in the north through circumstances or conflict with their parents. They sung on the buses which moved them in a mass migration from north to south in groups; some chewed their fingernails expectantly, all nervous to find out what their new home was like. When they waved at the South Sudanese who gathered to welcome them and were cheered as they took their first steps off the bus after the long ride, they realised they had the opportunity to create a new nation. Many started off with nothing in this new South Sudan, being unable to transport bricks and mortar from their northern homes and so were forced to spend their first nights under canvas, but nonetheless they didn't complain. It was a fresh start.

Instead of favouritism or fear, future partnership in hydrocarbon exploration, production and exploitation will be judged on merit and the benefit it has to the South Sudanese people. South Sudan does not come from a position of former servitude to the west like so many other African petrostates do; western companies cannot flex their muscles and remind states that they once were under their thrall. There can be no sense of entitlement to gas and oil anymore in South Sudan.

South Sudan is almost unique in Africa in that colonial celebratism is a moot argument: there has been no colonialism in South Sudan's untarnished history book to celebrate. There has likewise been no colonialism to apologise for. However there is still a need to be mindful of the threat of colonialism. Though it may not, unlike other nations which comprise the African lions that have such potential to dominate the world in the future, have a colonial past, it could – through mismanagement – have a colonial future. Salva Kiir, the President of the autonomous region of south Sudan prior to secession, Vice President of Sudan itself up to the moment of secession and likely President of the new nation of South Sudan, has, like Nigerian President Goodluck Jonathan, a unique sartorial calling card. Rarely is Kiir seen in public without a wide brimmed black cowboy hat. The hat was a gift from former US President George W Bush, and successive US envoys to Kiir as he has guided South Sudan to independence, including John Kerry in early January 2011, have continued the tradition of plying Kiir with an all-American ten gallon hat.

Philip Winter, a fellow of the Rift Valley Institute who has more than 35 years experience of dealing with the problems in Sudan, recognised that the future for South Sudan would be difficult. "But," he wrote, "consider where South Sudan was ten years ago - locked in an endless and fruitless civil war, with little hope on the horizon, and where it is now, brimming with optimism, bursting with trade, and benefiting from the return of the educated from the diaspora, excited by and intent on running the last lap through the referendum to statehood. The old order is over, the maps will be re-drawn and one can only wish the new order well as the people of South Sudan confront all the challenges of a new nation."[162]

With the newly redrawn and reprinted maps and the promises of a whole continent, never mind a nation on their shoulders, South Sudan will find it difficult to succeed. But if they do, then they will be the first country to have shaken off the shackles of colonialism and demonstrate through their overwhelmingly large oil and gas reserves the true potential of a continent of African lions that have for too long been kept caged by western gamekeepers.

Index

References

[1] African Development Bank and the African Union, Oil and Gas in Africa (July 2009)

[2] Compass, Nigeria loses $150 billion to gas flaring (17 January 2011)
http://www.compassnewspaper.com/NG/index.php?option=com_content&view=article&id=73400:nigeria-loses-150-billion-to-gas-flaring&catid=111:energy&Itemid=712

[3] PriceWaterhouseCoopers, Energy & Utilities: The African Oil & Gas Survey 2010 (August 2010)

[4] BBC News, Kenya corruption costs government dearly (3 December 2010) http://www.bbc.co.uk/news/world-africa-11913876

[5] BP, Statistical Review of World Energy 2010

[6] African Development Bank Group, Commodities Brief: Crude Oil and Natural Gas Production in Africa and the Global Market Situation (8 October 2010)

[7] Deutsche Bank, Oil & Gas for Beginners (9 September 2010)

[8] UPI, Gazprom looks for more LNG opportunities (8 December 2010) http://www.upi.com/Science_News/Resource-Wars/2010/12/08/Gazprom-looks-for-more-LNG-opportunities/UPI-69281291811096/

[9] ICIS-Heren ESGM, Shell to launch 'new strategy' in Algeria E&P efforts (2 December 2010)

[10] The Oxford Institute for Energy Studies, The Evolution and Functioning of the Traded Gas Market in Britain (August 2010)

[11] Business Monitor International, Nigeria Oil and Gas Report Q2 2010 (April 2010)

[12] Oil and Glory, Foreign Policy Magazine, Can Goodluck Jonathan survive Nigeria's oil wars? (30 November 2010)

http://oilandglory.foreignpolicy.com/posts/2010/11/30/can_goodl
uck_jonathan_survive_nigerias_oil_wars

[13] Bloomberg, Nigeria Oil Union on Strike at Exxon Unit to
Protest Employment Situation (2 December 2010)
http://www.bloomberg.com/news/2010-12-02/nigeria-oil-union-
on-indefinite-strike-at-exxon-mobil-unit.html

[14] IHS-CERA, Regas Terminal Inventory (14 September 2010)

[15] Personal interview with Nick Grealy (November 2010)

[16] Philip Rice & Patricia Waugh, Modern Literary Theory (2001)

[17] Edward Said, 'Two Visions of Heart of Darkness', Culture and
Imperialism (1993)

[18] The Guardian, Negative perceptions slow Africa's
development (10 December 2010)
http://www.guardian.co.uk/global-development/poverty-
matters/2010/dec/10/africa-postcolonial-perceptions

[19] The Guardian, US Embassy Cables: US monitors China and its
expanding role in Africa (8 December 2010)
http://www.guardian.co.uk/world/us-embassy-cables-
documents/250144

[20] Nigerian Compass, When will Nigeria attain 40b barrel oil
reserves? (22 November 2010)
http://www.compassnewspaper.com/NG/index.php?option=com
_content&view=article&id=70102:when-will-nigeria-attain-40b-
barrel-oil-reserves-&catid=111:energy&Itemid=712

[21] allAfrica.com, Nigeria: Audit of 120 Oil Blocks Delays 2010
Licensing Round (4 November 2010)
http://allafrica.com/stories/201011050608.html

[22] The Daily Independent, Oil: Nigerians in UK, others await PIB
passage, says High Commissioner (22 November 2010)
http://www.independentngonline.com/DailyIndependent/Articl
e.aspx?id=24239

[23] UPI, Gazprom holds off on Nigeria (19 November 2010) http://www.upi.com/Science_News/Resource-Wars/2010/11/19/Gazprom-holds-off-on-Nigeria/UPI-37901290176267/

[24] The Guardian, Nigeria feared coup as president lay dying overseas (8 December 2010) http://www.guardian.co.uk/world/2010/dec/08/wikileaks-cables-nigeria-president-death

[25] Chinua Achebe, The trouble with Nigeria (1984)

[26] Monocle, Style Leaders: Delta force – Nigeria (November 2010)

[27] Bloomberg, Petrobras Says Brazil May Import 40 Cargoes of LNG by Year-End (2 December 2010) http://noir.bloomberg.com/apps/news?pid=newsarchive&sid=ayOqvpCmd6KY

[28] International Maritime Bureau, Piracy and Armed Robbery Against Ships (October 2010)

[29] allAfrica.com, Nigeria: Niger Delta – 'JTF Won't Be Provoked to Declare War On Militants' (24 November 2010) http://allafrica.com/stories/201011250373.html

[30] BBC News, Nigeria's shadowy oil rebels (20 April 2006) http://news.bbc.co.uk/1/hi/world/africa/4732210.stm

[31] The Guardian, Goodluck Jonathan sworn in as Nigerian president (6 May 2010) http://www.guardian.co.uk/world/2010/may/06/goodluck-jonathan-nigeria-president

[32] Al-Jazeera, Nigeria military frees oil hostages (18 November 2010) http://english.aljazeera.net/news/africa/2010/11/2010111821051519243.html

[33] Reuters, Nigeria militants deny army raid in oil delta (22 November 2010)
http://af.reuters.com/article/topNews/idAFJOE6AL0D520101122

[34] International Maritime Bureau, Piracy and Armed Robbery Against Ships (January 2010)

[35] WikiLeaks, Nigeria: Shell briefs ambassador on oil gas issues, comments on President's health and high-level corruption (February 2009)
http://wikileaks.ch/cable/2009/02/09ABUJA259.html

[36] Bloomberg, Nigeria Oil Clashes Threaten Production in Challenge to Jonathan (28 November 2010)
http://www.bloomberg.com/news/2010-11-28/nigeria-oil-region-fighting-threatens-production-in-challenge-to-jonathan.html

[37] The New York Times, The Hostage Business (4 December 2009)
http://www.nytimes.com/2009/12/06/magazine/06kidnapping-t.html?pagewanted=all

[38] Vanguard, JTF impounds 13,800 litres of illegally refined petroleum products (20 December 2010)
http://allafrica.com/stories/201012210240.html

[39] Vanguard, How JTF subdued Togo (3 December 2010)
http://www.vanguardngr.com/2010/12/how-jtf-subdued-togo/

[40] Reuters, Civilians flee army raids in Nigerian oil delta (3 December 2010)
http://af.reuters.com/article/worldNews/idAFTRE6B26JU20101203?sp=true

[41] Vanguard, John Togo writes Obama on 'bloodbath' in Ayakoromor (3 December 2010)
http://www.vanguardngr.com/2010/12/john-togo-writes-obama-on-%E2%80%98bloodbath%E2%80%99-in-ayakoromor/

[42] United Nations, UN Human Development Report, Niger Delta (2006)

[43] allAfrica.com, Nigeria: Ex-Militant Blames Sea Pirates for Mobil Facility Attack (17 November 2010) http://allafrica.com/stories/201011180262.html

[44] Bloomberg, Nigerian Militant Okah Says No Military Solution in Oil-Rich Delta (6 December 2010)

[45] Chatham House, Nigeria-related financial crime and its links with Britain (November 2006)

[46] Transparency International UK, Corruption Perceptions Index 2010

[47] The Guardian, A Mexican, a Kiwi and a Nigerian walk into a bar... (4 December 2010) http://www.guardian.co.uk/world/2010/dec/04/global-sense-of-humour

[48] Chinua Achebe, No Longer at Ease (1960)

[49] BBC News, Shell and Halliburton quizzed over Nigeria 'corruption' (30 November 2010) http://www.bbc.co.uk/news/world-africa-11877434

[50] BBC News, Nigeria drops Dick Cheney bribery charges (17 December 2010) http://www.bbc.co.uk/news/world-africa-12018900

[51] Karl Maier, This House Has Fallen: Nigeria in crisis (2002)

[52] Mark Curtis, Unpeople: Britain's Secret Human Rights Abuses (2004)

[53] The New Criterion, The perils of activism: Ken Saro-Wiwa (January 2000)

[54] The New York Review of Books, The Case of Ken Saro-Wiwa (20 April 1995)

[55] The Independent on Sunday, Ken Saro-Wiwa was framed, secret evidence shows (5 December 2010) http://www.independent.co.uk/news/world/africa/ken-sarowiwa-was-framed-secret-evidence-shows-2151577.html

[56] EIA, Country Analysis Briefs: Nigeria (July 2010)

[57] BBC, QI Series 2 Episode 12: Birth (17 December 2004)

[58] allAfrica.com, Nigeria: Power Outage – FG Loses US$60 Million of LNG Cargoes (4 January 2011) http://allafrica.com/stories/201101050616.html

[59] Lorna Siggins, Once Upon a Time in the West: The Corrib Gas Controversy (September 2010)

[60] Der Spiegel, The Nigeria Report: A Cesspool of Corruption and Crime in the Niger Delta (10 December 2010) http://www.spiegel.de/international/world/0,1518,733880,00.html

[61] The New York Times, Left Behind: As Oil Riches Flow, Poor Village Cries Out (22 December 2002) http://www.nytimes.com/2002/12/22/world/left-behind-as-oil-riches-flow-poor-village-cries-out.html?pagewanted=all

[62] The Guardian, US Embassy Cables: US monitors China and its expanding role in Africa (8 December 2010) http://www.guardian.co.uk/world/us-embassy-cables-documents/250144

[63] David Greely, Goldman Sachs webcast: Energy Outlook 2011-2012 (7 December 2010)

[64] AP, China will further boost economic ties with Africa (23 December 2010) http://hosted.ap.org/dynamic/stories/A/AS_CHINA_AFRICA_RELATIONS?SITE=PASUN&SECTION=HOME&TEMPLATE=DEFAULT

[65] Der Spiegel, Investment with Strings Attached: Cables Reveal Resentment at Chinese Influence in Africa (9 December 2010) http://www.spiegel.de/international/world/0,1518,733870,00.html

[66] Transparency International, Global Corruption Barometer 2010 (9 December 2010)

[67] The Guardian, Shell's grip on Nigerian state revealed (8 December 2010)

[68] WikiLeaks, Nigeria: Shell briefs ambassador on oil gas issues, comments on President's health and high-level corruption (February 2009) http://wikileaks.ch/cable/2009/02/09ABUJA259.html

[69] Ali Mazrui, An African half-century (7 December 2010) http://www.guardian.co.uk/commentisfree/2010/dec/07/africa-century-postcolonial-independence

[70] OPEC, OPEC Bulletin (November 2010)

[71] The Financial Times, Africa: Oil & Gas – Special Report (28 January 2008)

[72] Wikileaks, Uganda: Tullow sees corruption in oil sale (9 December 2010) http://www.wikileaks.ch/cable/2009/12/09KAMPALA1401.html

[73] Daily Champion, SEC Boss Blames Nigeria's Economic Woes on Over Dependence on Oil (21 December 2010) http://allafrica.com/stories/201012210685.html

[74] BBC News, How Nigeria has affected the rest of Africa (30 September 2010) http://www.bbc.co.uk/news/world-africa-11429067

[75] The Africa Report, Banking on barrels (15 December 2010) http://www.theafricareport.com/investing-in-ghana/3318644-oil-a-gas-banking-on-barrels.html

[76] CIA, World Factbook: Ghana (January 2010)

[77] GhanaWeb, Regulating Ghana's Oil and Gas Sector: What should be the parameters? (18 January 2010)

[78] Africa Confidential, Confidential Agenda (23 November 2010)

[79] BBC News, Are Africa's commodities an economic blessing? (22 July 2010) http://www.bbc.co.uk/news/business-10710488

[80] The New York Times, Nigeria's Promise, Africa's Hope – Chinua Achebe (16 January 2011) http://www.nytimes.com/2011/01/16/opinion/16achebe.html?_r=1&pagewanted=all

[81] GhanaWeb, Is Ghana 'rehearsing' the resource curse? (2 December 2010) http://www.ghanaweb.com/GhanaHomePage/NewsArchive/artikel.php?ID=198555&comment=0#com

[82] EITI, Cameroon, Gabon, Kyrgyzstan and Nigeria designated as EITI Candidate countries that are "close to compliance" (26 October 2010) http://eiti.org/news-events/cameroon-gabon-kyrgyzstan-and-nigeria-designated-eiti-candidate-countries-are-close-comp

[83] NEITI, World Bank Backs NEITI (3 December 2010)

[84] Ghanaian Ministry for Energy, The Emerging Oil and Gas Sector: Policy Challenges (18 June 2010)

[85] The Financial Times, China's lending hits new heights (17 January 2011) http://www.ft.com/cms/s/0/488c60f4-2281-11e0-b6a2-00144feab49a.html?ftcamp=rss#axzz1BNKfslJt

[86] Edward Said, 'Two Visions of Heart of Darkness', Culture and Imperialism (1993)

[87] David Greely, Goldman Sachs webcast: Energy Outlook 2011-2012 (7 December 2010)

[88] Reuters, Ghana backs oil revenue collateral law (9 December 2010) http://af.reuters.com/article/investingNews/idAFJOE6B80O220101209

[89] The Guardian, Ghanaian MPs get a 17% pay rise and free laptop to improve democracy (20 October 2010)

http://www.guardian.co.uk/world/2010/oct/20/ghana-mps-pay-rise

[90] Ghana News Agency, Dr Chambas calls on Ghana to distribute oil wealth judiciously (29 November 2010) http://www.ghananewsagency.org/s_social/r_23009/

[91] BBC News, How the net connected the world (2 December 2010) http://www.bbc.co.uk/news/technology-11864350

[92] Author's personal correspondence

[93] Al-Jazeera, Riz Khan: When honour meets morality (30 November 2010)

[94] Al-Jazeera, China: A force for peace in Sudan? (11 January 2011) http://english.aljazeera.net/indepth/features/2011/01/2011191035 7773378.html

[95] GhanaWeb, Oil Companies Impose Foreign Policy on Ghana (2 December 2010) http://www.ghanaweb.com/GhanaHomePage/NewsArchive/arti kel.php?ID=198636

[96] Ghanaian Ministry for Energy, The Emerging Oil and Gas Sector: Policy Challenges (18 June 2010)

[97] Speech by President Barack Obama in Accra, Ghana (11 July 2010) http://www.ibtimes.com/articles/20090711/obamas-speech-accra-ghana-july-11-text.htm

[98] Tullow, Interview with Dai Jones (22 November 2010) http://www.tullowoil.com/Ghana/index.asp?pageid=55

[99] BBC News, Ghana oil begins pumping for first time (15 December 2010) http://www.bbc.co.uk/news/world-africa-11996983

[100] Reuters, Ghana sells its first crude oil exports to Exxon (12 January 2011)

http://af.reuters.com/article/investingNews/idAFJOE70B0G02011
0112

[101] The Financial Times, Ghana enters new era with oil field
launch (15 December 2010) http://www.ft.com/cms/s/0/2a785790-
0877-11e0-80d9-00144feabdc0.html

[102] GhanaWeb, Ghana becomes an oil nation (15 December 2010)
http://www.ghanaweb.com/GhanaHomePage/NewsArchive/arti
kel.php?ID=199503

[103] The Will, LPPC Bars Aondoakaa From Use of SAN (6
December 2010) http://thewillnigeria.com/politics/6794-LPPC-
Bars-Aondoakaa-From-Use-SAN.html

[104] Chatham House, Nigeria-related financial crime and its links
with Britain (November 2006)

[105] Bloomberg Businessweek, Shell Bribes Among 'Culture of
Corruption,' Panalpina Admits (5 November 2010)
http://www.businessweek.com/news/2010-11-05/shell-bribes-
among-culture-of-corruption-panalpina-admits.html

[106] The Guardian, The rhetoric of corporate social responsibility
outweighs the reality (11 October 2010)
http://www.guardian.co.uk/global-development/poverty-
matters/2010/oct/11/corporate-social-responsibility-africa-
progress

[107] allAfrica.com, Oil Firm Total E&P Finances Environmental
Projects (18 December 2010)
http://allafrica.com/stories/201012200178.html

[108] AP, China will further boost economic ties with Africa (23
December 2010)
http://hosted.ap.org/dynamic/stories/A/AS_CHINA_AFRICA_R
ELATIONS?SITE=PASUN&SECTION=HOME&TEMPLATE=DE
FAULT

[109] Wikileaks, Nigeria: Chinese Oil Companies Not So Welcome in Nigeria's (December 2009) http://wikileaks.ch/cable/2009/12/09ABUJA2170.html

[110] Chinese State Council Information Office, China-Africa Economic and Trade Cooperation (23 December 2010) http://news.xinhuanet.com/english2010/china/2010-12/23/c_13661632.htm

[111] Magharebia, Total to test Mauritania hydrocarbon discoveries (29 September 2010) http://www.magharebia.com/cocoon/awi/xhtml1/en_GB/features/awi/newsbriefs/general/2010/09/29/newsbrief-05

[112] The Guardian, Mauritania tries to close its borders (8 June 2010) http://www.guardian.co.uk/world/2010/jun/08/mauritania-closing-borders-al-qaida

[113] The Economist, Operational risk ratings 2010

[114] Max de Vietri, Mauritania's socio-political environment and its influence on the country's nascent petroleum industry (May 2009)

[115] EIA, Country Analysis Briefs: Angola (January 2010)

[116] The Guardian, Oil rich, dirt poor (26 August 2004) http://www.guardian.co.uk/politics/2004/aug/26/uk.world1

[117] The Progress Report, Friendly Dealings with Dictators (2004)

[118] OPEC, Monthly Oil Market Report (November 2010)

[119] IEA, Angola: Towards an Energy Strategy (2006)

[120] CCFD, Biens mal acquis… profitent trop souvent: La fortune des dictateurs et les complaisances occidentals (March 2007)

[121] Business Monitor International, Angola Oil and Gas Report Q4 2010 (September 2010)

[122] allAfrica, Total E&P Angola Pledges to Contain HIV/Aids (3 December 2010) http://allafrica.com/stories/201012060282.html

123 allAfrica, Oil Company Inspects Land Reserve for New Urban Centre (5 December 2010) http://allafrica.com/stories/201012060128.html

124 GhanaWeb, Democracy drives oil debates in Ghana (6 December 2010) http://www.ghanaweb.com/GhanaHomePage/NewsArchive/arti kel.php?ID=198883

125 Human Rights Watch, 'Letter from ExxonMobil', Well Oiled: Oil and Human Rights in Equatorial Guinea (July 2009)

126 allAfrica, Equatorial Guinea: Human Rights Drowning in Oil (25 August 2010) http://allafrica.com/stories/201008250008.html

127 The New York Times, Oil Corruption in Equatorial Guinea (9 July 2009) http://green.blogs.nytimes.com/2009/07/09/oil-corruption-in-equatorial-guinea/

128 Human Rights Watch, Well Oiled: Oil and Human Rights in Equatorial Guinea (July 2009)

129 The Independent, Teodoro Obiang Nguema: A brutal, bizarre jailer (13 May 2007)

130 AFP, Equatorial Guinea State Radio Hails President as Country's God (24 July 2003)

131 Reporters Sans Frontieres, Press Freedom Index 2010 (October 2010)

132 EITI, Letter to President Obiang (29 April 2010)

133 CIA, World Factbook (2010)

134 IMF, Equatorial Guinea Staff Report (17 October 2008)

135 CIA, World Factbook: Angola (2010)

136 Human Rights Watch, Some Transparency, No Accountability (12 January 2004)

137 Human Rights Watch, Transparency and Accountability in Angola (April 2010)

[138] OPEC, Monthly Oil Market Report (November 2010)

[139] The Guardian, Europe and Africa: a partnership of equals? (3 December 2010) http://www.guardian.co.uk/global-development/poverty-matters/2010/dec/03/europe-africa-ties-trade-aid-partnership

[140] Al-Jazeera, Riz Khan: What next for South Sudan? (3 January 2011)

[141] Pulitzer Centre, Southern Sudanese Independence: High Hopes, Huge Obstacles (28 November 2010) http://pulitzercenter.org/articles/southern-sudanese-say-independence-vote-will-improve-life

[142] Sudan Tribune, South Plans to Build Three Oil Refineries After Secession – Official (9 November 2010) http://allafrica.com/stories/201012070595.html

[143] Al-Jazeera, Sudan 'could give up' southern oil (17 December 2010) http://english.aljazeera.net/news/africa/2010/12/2010121721529930662.html

[144] Speech by President Barack Obama in Accra, Ghana (11 July 2010) http://www.ibtimes.com/articles/20090711/obamas-speech-accra-ghana-july-11-text.htm

[145] SP, Sharon Gesthuizen in Nigeria: Dag 1, Lagos (19 December 2010) http://www.sp.nl/wereld/nieuwsberichten/8258/101219-sharon_gesthuizen_in_nigeria_dag_1_lagos.html

[146] SP, Sharon Gesthuizen in Nigeria: Dag 2, Shell (20 December 2010) http://www.sp.nl/wereld/nieuwsberichten/8262/101220-sharon_gesthuizen_in_nigeria_dag_2_shell.html

[147] SP, Sharon Gesthuizen in Nigeria: Dag 3, Port Harcourt (21 December 2010) http://www.sp.nl/wereld/nieuwsberichten/8262/101220-sharon_gesthuizen_in_nigeria_dag_2_shell.html

[148] Global Witness, Crude Calculations (6 January 2011)
http://www.globalwitness.org/crudecalculationspress

[149] Al-Jazeera, China: A force for peace in Sudan? (11 January 2011)
http://english.aljazeera.net/indepth/features/2011/01/2011191035
7773378.html

[150] The Guardian, Peace at last: Gordon Brown on life after Downing Street (4 December 2010)
http://www.guardian.co.uk/politics/2010/dec/04/gordon-brown-interview

[151] Speech by the Right Hon Gordon Brown MP to African leaders, Kampala (24 July 2010)
http://www.gordonbrown.org.uk

[152] The Guardian, US embassy cables: African countries prefer Chinese aid to US-China cooperation (4 December 2010)
http://www.guardian.co.uk/world/us-embassy-cables-documents/248299

[153] The Guardian, US embassy cables: Nicolas Sarkozy's personal diplomacy in Africa is hamfisted (30 November 2010)
http://www.guardian.co.uk/world/us-embassy-cables-documents/165955

[154] Financial Times, Perenco looks to Nigeria for next phase (9 January 2011) http://www.ft.com/cms/s/0/acdafc16-1c0d-11e0-9b56-00144feab49a.html#axzz1AcaYoCn4

[155] Oil and Glory, Foreign Policy Magazine, Tom Bower's Oil (7 December 2010)
http://oilandglory.foreignpolicy.com/posts/2010/12/07/og_book_review_tom_bowers_oil

[156] OREA, Managing Oil Revenue in Uganda: A Policy Note (March 2009)

[157] Chatham House, Nigeria-related financial crime and its links with Britain (November 2006)

[158] Speech by Hillary Clinton to the Corporate Council on Africa's Seventh Biennial US-Africa Business Summit (1 October 2009)

[159] Al-Jazeera, Sudan vote 'peaceful and credible' (17 January 2011) http://english.aljazeera.net/news/africa/2011/01/201111791938988 874.html

[160] Al-Jazeera, Riz Khan: What next for South Sudan? (3 January 2011)

[161] allAfrica.com, Sudan: South Expects New Oil Finds to Boost Its Economy (13 January 2011) http://allafrica.com/stories/201101140242.html

[162] Royal African Society, A new player in a multi-polar world (December 2010) http://royalafricansociety.org/index.php?option=com_content&t ask=view&id=752

Printed in Great Britain
by Amazon.co.uk, Ltd.,
Marston Gate.